MW01614713

People are feeling great on the Full Body Cleanse!!!

I am on Day 17 and so far, so great! I am down 6-1/2 pounds and feel great. I have more energy and I am sleeping better. The recipes have been easy to follow and delicious. I am eating many foods I have never tried and enjoying them.

Thanks!!
Lori S.

The Plan: I loved that each day was detailed and written out, it took the decision making out of my hands and was freeing in a way. We immediately loved the new breakfast foods. Arash and I both felt great, had loads of energy and felt the herbs doing their work while eating a clean, healthy diet. This cleanse is a way of life and has and kept us mindful as we reset some of the habits which had crept up. Uttara N.

My favorite recipes were the lunches that combined a grain (for me quinoa) and veggies, fruits, nuts, beans, etc. Those were wonderful and delicious, and presented a new way of approaching lunch that I hadn't considered before. I believe I felt the best I've ever felt that month on the cleanse
Connie S.

The first week is over and I feel great. I feel lighter more energized. The meals are so filling that I don't snack at all. I don't have any craving for sugar. I have lost 3 pounds. Ekta G.

I enjoyed the 30 day Vegan Cleanse! The food was delicious and it became easier to follow the plan once I got started and gathered ingredients weekly.

I began to feel great and for me, giving up sugar and eating a healthier plant based diet was important. I continue to incorporate many of the recipes in my diet and look forward to repeating the cleanse again.
Susan H.

I jumped into the 30 Day Vegan Full Body Cleanse because I wanted to lose weight in a totally health-conscious way. The promise of more energy, reduced inflammation and other health benefits was also very appealing. I stuck to the plan completely for the entire 30 days, taking my herbs daily, and refraining from coffee, alcohol, sugar, and animal proteins. The recipes in this plan are amazing. The plan lays out what you will need very well, by providing helpful tips on what to prepare for the next day's meal. Shopping is also made easier with the handy lists of ingredients. The author's "personal favorites" were also helpful. After sticking to the plan for 30 days, I felt lighter all over, and my body felt healthy in every way. My energy was great, and my skin and hair looked fantastic.
Terry N.

I have never been interested in a vegan way of life. However, after Ahnjel's cleanse, that changed. Her tasty recipes and recommended foods have become a way of life for me. I lost weight, but more importantly, I have been able to maintain the weight loss by continuing to eat her recommended foods and recipes. My complexion glowed and was even noticed by strangers! As I continue to make these healthy eating choices, my body feels clean and healthy!
Susan K.

Full Body
30 Day Vegan Cleanse

Full Body
30 Day Vegan Cleanse

Ahnjel Ali

Body Mind Spirit Publishing Group
Culver City, California

Notice: If you have a corn allergy, do not take these herbs. (They are processed with corn starch.)

Disclaimer

This book is not a medical manual. It is intended as a reference for a healthy lifestyle. The information is given to help you make informed choices about your health. This Cleanse is not meant as a substitute for any treatment that may have been prescribed by your doctor. If you suspect that you have a medical problem, you are urged to seek competent medical help.

If you are pregnant or nursing, it is recommended that you do NOT do this Cleanse. This is not the appropriate time to make radical changes to your body. These herbal formulas are NOT to be used by a pregnant woman.

All recommendations are believed to be effective, but since the actual use of herbs by others is beyond the control of the author, no expressed or implied guarantee as to the effects of their use can be given nor liability taken. The publisher and author expressly disclaim all liability connected with goods/services/ products obtained with this Cleanse. Any use of the information in this book is at the reader's discretion.

Do not stop taking any medications your doctor has you on.

Cover photo: courtesy of William Short
Cover Model: Ahnjel Ali

Explanation of yoga pose on the cover: For years now, whenever I have my yoga class in Eagle pose I am reminded of the double-helix DNA strand. I chose this pose for the cover because the foods we eat do affect our DNA. Studies have shown how our DNA is altered by years of eating processed foods with their additives and preservatives. I know that by eating natural foods, our DNA remains healthy, our bodies thrive, and our lives are better for it.

ISBN 978-0-9856899-0-2

First published in the United States, 2012
Body Mind Spirit Publishing Group®

It is easy to feel how great and beautiful life is when you feel wonderful every day!

Ahnjel Ali does this by teaching people to bring healthy balance into their lives. Ahnjel has 20 years of experience as a licensed Acupuncturist/Herbalist in California. She is also a Certified Sports Nutritionist. Ahnjel has 30 years' experience in the fitness industry, and teaches yoga. Ahnjel's Husband, Majid Ali, is also a licensed Acupuncturist/Herbalist and a Certified Sports Nutritionist. Together they are raising two beautiful boys and teaching them how to have healthy and very happy lives!

Acknowledgments:

I am sincerely happy to say that this book will be out just in time for my 50th birthday! It has been a wonderful 50 years, thanks to many people. I have always felt life was an adventure, and I thank my husband, Majid Ali, for being adventurous enough to spend many wonderful years with me; and for being one of my greatest teachers! I sincerely thank my two amazing and joyful boys for all they have brought into my life and all they have taught me.

I am very thankful to my friends who did this Cleanse and had wonderful feedback for me.

I am thankful to William Short for being generous with his time and his professional experience in taking the cover photo.

I am thankful for Terry Nozick for her generosity with her time and professional expertise in editing this book.

I am sincerely thankful for all the people in my life who are helping me to become a better human being all the time.

Welcome to what I sincerely hope will be the rest of your life!

30-Day Full-Body Vegan Cleanse

Why Should I Do a Full-Body Cleanse?

You should do a full-body cleanse because your life is worth it. You are worth more than taking pills for several decades and being unable to enjoy your life because of health problems.

You should do a full body cleanse if you eat the Standard American Diet, also known as SAD. If you eat the SAD way, you either already have one or more of the chronic diseases very prevalent in America, or you will have one. This is not an opinion, it is a fact.

One hundred percent of the people eating the SAD will end up with one or more of the following chronic health conditions: heart disease, hypertension, cancer, stroke, diabetes, kidney disease, lung disease. Volumes of research have proven that each of these is almost completely preventable, and that each happens as a direct result of eating the SAD.

Need More Reasons?

On this Full-Body Cleanse you will:
- Lose weight
- Avoid or stop Metabolic Syndrome
- Reduce your blood pressure
- Reduce your cholesterol
- Reduce your blood glucose level
- Reduce inflammation throughout your body
- Help reduce arthritis symptoms
- Help reduce allergies

Help Strengthen Your Immune System

A direct result of eating foods filled with nutrients that are only beneficial to your body is a strengthened immune system. The other side of this statement is that, on the Cleanse, you will not be eating foods that are harmful to your body. Every food in this 30-Day Cleanse gives your body nutrients that it needs to maintain health. Every cell in your body will benefit. This is all in absolute contrast to eating processed foods that are filled with man-made chemicals that your liver cannot easily break-down. And processed foods give your body no useful nutrients at all. Processed foods are not just causing your liver to work harder, they are hard on your immune system, spleen, large and small intestines, kidneys, and vascular system, which means, ultimately, more work for your heart. This information alone should cause people to want to radically change their diets.

This Full-Body Vegan Cleanse can help dramatically with autoimmune conditions because it reduces inflammation in the body. All autoimmune conditions have an inflammatory aspect. The foods on this Cleanse are **only** helpful to your immune system, and can be thought of as building blocks for what your immune system needs to function at it absolute best, the way it is supposed to. Removing foods from your diet that are unnatural or processed with man-made chemicals will reduce the work your immune system has to do. An autoimmune condition is caused by an over-reactive system.

All of these effects are fully supported and enhanced by the herbs you will be taking.

Feel Better Every Day!

May this be your jump-start to a better life

My hope is that by starting this 30-day plan, you will change your life for the better! Once you complete this plan you will feel so good, that you will continue to make better choices throughout your life.

You can do this! All it takes is your willingness and your commitment to yourself.

What Makes This Cleanse Different From Others?

Eating vegan is a very healthy way to go through life, and by adopting this system of eating you will become healthier. But, if you haven't been vegan up to this point in your life, this 30-Day Full-Body Vegan Cleanse makes even deeper changes throughout your body because of the addition of the herbal formulas. These herbs will eliminate any unhealthy build-up in your body that is affecting your immune system, liver, kidneys, intestinal tract, and even your brain.

For those of you who are already vegans, this Cleanse can still be of great benefit because of the herbal formulas. If you are already vegan, you know how beneficial plant foods are for you. Herbs are very potent in their effects and make amazing changes to our bodies.

These herbal formulas will make a difference that you will be able to feel. Taking them will start to change some of the negative things done to your organs. This Cleanse together with these herbs will make a difference to the health of your lymph system, intestinal tract, liver, kidneys, immune system, vascular system, and your brain – all these organs will benefit.

This Is the Healthiest Way to Lose Weight

Bringing this Cleanse into your life is the truly healthiest way to lose weight. It's not meant to be a quick fix, as quick fixes to eating do not encompass health. This Cleanse is a lifestyle. There will never be a replacement for what it takes to build a healthy human body. There are no drugs that will ever give you a healthy body.

The foods in this Cleanse are truly foods you can eat the rest of your life. It is not a system of counting calories. There will be no need to count calories if you are eating the foods suggested here. This system will not suggest unhealthy foods, like many of the big weight-loss systems on the market. Nor does this system suggest you can eat anything you want and still lose weight. The reality is if you are eating foods with sugar and numerous man-made chemicals, your body will truly never be healthy.

What Makes This a Full-Body Cleanse?

Along with eating vegan for a full 30 days, with this Cleanse you get 28 days' worth of herbs to clear different levels of your body each week. This part of the Cleanse is done in a very meticulous way, starting with a more superficial layer and each week progressing into deeper layers of your body.

The first week of herbs are meant to clear your lymph system. Yes, your lymph system is always processing stuff, but these herbs will greatly assist your entire lymph system in clearing out your lymph nodes. Even this first week of herbs will make a quantitative difference to your immune system.

The second week of herbs is meant to clear out the intestinal tract. For everybody with intestinal symptoms, this week will make a huge difference, whether these problems are gas, bloating, constipation, diarrhea, or even irritable bowel syndrome (IBS). This herbal
formula will reduce all of these problems and reduce the inflammation in your intestinal tract. This week will also be a big help to your immune system. There is constant communication between your immune system and your digestive tract; there has to be in order to survive and get rid of pathogenic bacteria that shouldn't be in your intestinal tract, (and yet still allow the healthy bacterial strains to stay). If disease-causing bacteria are housed in your intestines, your immune system is kept very busy.

The third week of herbs will clean out the liver. From the time we are born, the liver has a very hard job. It has to break down all carbohydrates, fats, and even proteins we consume. The liver is also responsible for breaking down the numerous man-made chemicals we ingest, the chemicals we breathe in, and all medications taken. This has been a huge job, on a 24-hour basis, since your birth! The herbs in this formula will support your liver in all it does, and promote healthy liver functioning.

The final week is to cleanse the kidneys, the final filtering system for our bodies. The kidneys filter out of our bodies what is not needed, in the form of urine. The kidneys also retain whatever minerals,
vitamins, and trace elements the body needs. All man-made chemicals (preservatives, food additives, medications, air-borne chemicals), get filtered through the kidneys and are a huge burden to them.

What Should I Expect?

As you go through this Cleanse, there are a lot of changes that will be happening to your body. Although every individual will have his/her own personal experience with this, every person will get some of the changes that are possible. You will see some changes and feel others. Some changes you may not see or feel at all, but they will show up in your blood work.

By adopting this way of eating for a longer period of time you will get more of these changes to your body.

Changes you will see include:
- A definite weight loss
- An improvement in your skin
- Healthier and shinier hair

Changes you will feel include:
- More energy
- Clearer thinking
- Reduced or eliminated gas/bloating/constipation/diarrhea
- Reduction in allergy symptoms
- A reduction or elimination of headaches or even migraines
- A reduction or elimination of body aches
- Reduction in PMS

Changes you will see on blood work include:
- Lower blood glucose levels
- Lower cholesterol
- Lower triglycerides
- Reduced antibodies
- Reduced C-reactive protein/inflammatory marker

One more important medical change:
- Lower blood pressure

Changes That Will Make You Feel Better

During the 30 days of this Full-Body Cleanse, by eliminating wheat, dairy products, and processed sugar from your diet, you will notice definite changes in several aspects of your body. One of the first differences you may notice is in how much better you feel overall. This Cleanse will allow you to make a big difference to any digestive issues you may have. If you often have gas/bloating, you will notice a big improvement. If you suffer daily headaches, this Full-Body Cleanse will most likely make changes to those. If you suffer from daily or repeated sinus infections, you will most likely notice an improvement. You may notice a lessening of allergy symptoms. And for women, there should be a reduction of any PMS, or menstrual cramping. (If you continue with this way of eating, you can practically eliminate those issues.)

How Much Time Does Meal Prep Take?

The meals in this plan do not require more time than cooking regular meals. However, there is a difference if you consider the time taken to heat a pre-made processed meal that is full of sodium, preservatives, and other unnatural ingredients that not only cause health problems, but give your body nothing healthful in return for the money you spend on them. There is preparation time, including cutting of vegetables and fruits. But this is a much better way to spend your time and your money.

It is always important to plan ahead. This is a very important step to eating healthy, making sure you don't get stuck in the situation of needing to grab fast food for lunch or dinner out of desperation.

There are **Time-Saving Tips** provided for many of the meals, which will help you to be able to eat healthfully and stick to this Full-Body Cleanse.

Foods to Avoid While on the Cleanse

You are perfectly capable of taking some foods out of your diet for 30 days. Let's put this in perspective: Most likely, you are over the age of 10, which means you have been living for a few decades, a good number of years, many months, and thousands of days. This Cleanse is just 30 days. That's a relatively short timeframe. So for just 30 days, enjoy your life without:
- Alcohol
- Dairy products
- Coffee
- Sugar
- Wheat

Substitutes are listed on the Shopping List at the end.

Even More Reasons ...

The Centers for Disease Control and Prevention (CDC) has a Web site with great information about America's health and how our health has changed. This Web site is full of useful – and horrifying – statistics on obesity rates and associated health problems over several decades among the America population. Just reading this Web site should be enough to make people change their lifestyle.

According to the CDC, statistics for obesity reveal that in 1985, there were 14 states with an obesity rate less than 10 percent; eight states had an obesity rate of 10 percent to 14 percent; 28 states were not recorded. Fast forward to 2010 and EVERY state has an obesity rate above 20 percent! I am going to say this again because it is dramatic. **EVERY state has an obesity rate above 20 percent!**

Fourteen states have an obesity rate of 20 percent to 24 percent; 23 states have an obesity rate of 25 percent to 29 percent; 13 states have an obesity rate above 29 percent. There was no such thing in 1985 and certainly not in the late fifties and early sixties when many of us were born!

Currently, every state has an obesity rate above 15 percent. For 2010, not one state in the United States reached the goal set by the Healthy People 2010 movement to reduce the obesity rate to below 15%. As of now, there is not one state that has only 15 percent of its population listed as obese with all its concurrent health problems. There is absolutely no denying that this is due to the unnatural, processed foods being eaten as well as inactive lifestyles.

If you have kids, there are numerous reasons to do this Cleanse, and bring these healthy changes to your family. You want to be able to stay healthy to enjoy all the wonderful things your kids do. The healthier you are, the less your kids will have to worry about you. And your health becomes more vital as you age. Keeping your family healthy should be one of your top priorities.

Currently, there are fast rising numbers of children developing Type II Diabetes. Diabetes Type II used to be diagnosed only in adults, usually after the age of 40. Now, because of the foods being eaten, children are commonly diagnosed with it. The diagnosis of children with Type II Diabetes has consistently and dramatically climbed in the last three decades. Currently, for every three cases of Type II Diabetes being diagnosed, one is in a child. Kids with diabetes are not as easily treated with the available drugs. The reasons for this are beyond the scope of this Cleanse, but it all starts with how the human body is trained.

What Are Your Reasons for Doing This Full-Body Cleanse?

"Motivation is what gets you started. Habit is what keeps you going."– Former runner Jim Ryun
Know what your motivation is. If you can see that, you will be able to retain it and it will keep you going through these 30 days. Take just a few minutes and write down your motivation. Your written words will always be there for you.

_____
_____
_____
_____
_____
_____
_____
_____
_____
_____

Helpful Tips Before Starting

- First of all, be kind to yourself while you go through this 30-Day Full-Body Cleanse. If eating this way is very new to you, be patient. You have chosen to do this as a great way to take care of yourself. Allow yourself to learn this way of eating; do not expect to instantly know it. Eating like this is very doable and you are capable of doing it. Just have the mindset that it is a learning process.

- On weekends it would always be helpful to look at the week ahead so you know what to expect. Doing some prep work over the weekend might make these 30 days easier for you. For example, look ahead at the meals for the week and take the time to buy the groceries you will need.
- Start every morning with a 12-ounce glass of water.
- Aim to drink a minimum of two liters of water every day. The ultimate goal would be to drink three liters of water daily. This is important for your body always, but especially while on this Full-Body Cleanse
- If you want something else to drink when you are eating your breakfast, choose an herbal, black, mint, or chamomile tea. Black tea is very good for your digestive tract, and helps make you alkaline. Another excellent choice is green tea, which is great for your liver, helps reduce cholesterol, helps keep you more alkaline, and stimulates your immune system.
- Options are always great, so if there is a particular meal that you really enjoyed, feel free to have it again in place of something else. Also, if you see an upcoming meal that you know you will not like, replace it with another that you will like.
- **"Time-Saving Tips"** are listed in a number of places. If these can help you, and still allow you to stick to this

Vegan Cleanse, then take the option. A cleanse doesn't have to be hard on your schedule, but to get the results you want, consistently sticking to the Cleanse is what matters most at the end of the day.

- It is recommended that you snack between your meals IF you are hungry. If you know your blood sugar levels drop causing you to feel "starved," it is much better to snack on something healthy than to grab foods not in this Cleanse. When someone feels starved, they have a tendency to grab for processed foods loaded with sugar, salt, and fats. By always planning ahead, you can avoid this pitfall. Plan ahead and bring the right foods with you.

- For all the recipes calling for olive oil, the best choice is "extra-virgin olive oil," which is the highest quality olive oil produced. It is mechanically pressed and no chemicals or solvents are used in its production. Extra-virgin olive oil is from the first pressing of the olives, so it therefore yields an oil rich in phytochemicals and antioxidants. It must adhere to certain free fatty-acid specifications, flavor, and odor in order to be termed "extra-virgin olive oil."

- The grains you will be eating while on this Full-Body Cleanse are what are called "ancient grains," meaning they were used by ancient societies. For instance, kamut was used by early Egyptians. Quinoa was a consistent part of the South American diet 5,000 years ago, and provided numerous nutritional benefits. The Incas ate Quinoa regularly. Amaranth was eaten by people in South America and Central America as long as 8,000 years ago. It was a diet staple for the Aztecs, and was believed to confer an amazing strength to the people.

- It can be daunting to take on a new way of eating. To help you be successful and use your time, a number of meals were placed as they are so that you could make extra servings of grains, beans, or vegetables to be able to use in a meal two to four days later.

And Most Importantly ...

- **All of the breakfasts on the Cleanse are single serving. They are fast and easy to make, while being calorie loaded enough to start your day and still be very healthy for you.**
- **Lunches are also single serving. The majority were also designed to be easy, quick, and packable, although a few require a little more prep time. Looking ahead will help you in this regard so that you can be set up to bring the lunch with you. If a lunch is not doable for your schedule, you of course have the option to choose one that will work for you.**
- **Most of the dinner recipes are large enough to serve four people. If you won't need as much, cut each recipe in half.**
- **If you do cook larger amounts than you will be eating for dinner, use some of the leftovers for your next day's lunch. Make a note of any lunch recipe that you skip, and try it another day.**
- **All of the salad dressing recipes are printed on the first day you will use them, and also at the end for easy reference.**

- It is helpful to have some of the salad dressings already made and stored in the refrigerator. They usually can store for up to two weeks.
- Realizing that we all have busy lives, and cooking like this may be a new way of taking care of yourself and your family, I put in close proximity days where you might be using some of the same ingredients. For example, grains. If you are cooking grains one day, there is a "Time-Saving Tip" to cook extra for a recipe that follows one to three days later.

Taking It up a Notch!

It would be a great addition to this Cleanse to drink a green vegetable juice every day. You can play with it so that it works for you. If you want a green juice every day, you will definitely see and feel the difference it makes to your body. If every day is too much, then make it three to five days a week. Even when you are finished with the Cleanse, this is a very healthful way to continue to get some vegetables into your diet. It truly makes a huge difference to your body.

A great daily green juice and my favorite is a mix of spinach, celery, parsley, radishes, and garlic. I use a Vitamix® to get all the nutrients from the entire plant- all the fiber, all the nutrients. Better than a juicer, a Vitamix® is an extremely powerful blender that shreds everything you put into it. A juicer extracts the water and only some of the nutrients from the vegetables, and none of the fiber. With a Vitamix® you will be getting all of the spinach, celery, parsley, radishes, and garlic you put into the machine, just in a drinkable, puréed version. For your time, your money spent on vegetables, and for your health, a Vitamix® will make a much bigger difference to your body than a juicer.

While a deep green vegetable juice daily is definitely the best choice, there are a number of different juices listed at the end of this Cleanse. It would be great to try a few different ones while on the Cleanse since this may be a new chapter in your life. Experiment!

If you would like to order a Vitamix® visit www.vitamix .com or call +1 800-848-2649. You can get free ground shipping by using the code 06-00749. That will be a savings of $25.00.

More Restrictions, If You Want

Many people experience inflammation and immune reactions to a number of different foods. If your body is sensitive to certain foods, anytime you eat those foods your body has an inflammatory reaction. Some of the very common foods that cause reactions are gluten, soy, corn, and the nightshade group of vegetables (tomatoes, potatoes, bell peppers, eggplant). If you suspect that any of these common food irritants are problematic for you, this would be a great time to eliminate them.

For the general population, this Cleanse does not eliminate these foods. Soy is not specifically called for in any of the recipes, but it is an option that can be used in the form of tofu, soy milk, or soy yogurt. Corn is not used in many of the recipes and can be avoided during this Cleanse, but the herbs do have some corn starch on them. The nightshade vegetables are used in a number of recipes. You can replace these with a different vegetable or completely skip these recipes.

This Cleanse is wheat-free, but not completely gluten-free. Some recipes call for barley or soy sauce, which contain gluten. If you want to be completely gluten-free, replace the barley with millet, quinoa, or another grain, and replace the soy sauce with tamari sauce.

A friend of mine who did the Cleanse and that does have reactions to gluten, soy, corn and the nightshade group eliminated these foods also while she did the Cleanse. Once she took these foods out of her diet, all her aches and pains went away. And by the third day of the Cleanse, she no longer had headaches which she had been experiencing several times a week, and her migraines went away while she was on the Cleanse.

I Want You to Know …

That eating healthy does not mean eating rabbit food. Eating healthy does not mean you have to eat and suffer through terrible foods without flavor.

I would sincerely like this to be the first step for you to eat healthy for the rest of your life and the only way a person can do that is if they have variety. The variety of foods that come in all the different colors supplies your body with the range of phytonutrients it needs.

I am big on options, as you will see. With so many options, you can make choices so that this 30-Day Full-Body Vegan Cleanse will work for you. Replace any meal you want with a meal you would rather have, whether as a taste preference or a matter of time and convenience.

If You Need Proof of What This Can Do for You

While on this cleanse, you will most likely feel great. But, for some people, they want proof of what is going on inside their body to confirm any real physical benefits from eating so wisely. I encourage you to run blood tests. Run one blood test before you take this Cleanse and run one afterwards. Compare your outcomes for cholesterol, triglycerides, glucose levels, and especially C-reactive protein. If you have an autoimmune condition, run any previous test you have taken before showing alterations in antibodies. Depending on your situation, these could be Ig-A, Ig-E, Ig-G, or ANA. You would definitely see a bigger difference in the range of your results if you eat this vegan menu for three months.

I encourage you to write down how you are feeling while you are doing this Full-Body Cleanse.

This is an important step in your path to making this commitment to yourself because, most likely, this Full-Body Cleanse will have you feeling better than you have felt in years. The brain is absolutely amazing, but our perceptions do get altered over time. By writing it down, you will always have your experience and changes as a reference. To make this easy, space has been created for you to make these notes at the end of each day.

Set Yourself Up for Success

This Full-Body Cleanse is doable! I want you to be successful, but most importantly, set *yourself* up for success. The following three steps are your keys to success:

1. Look ahead at the week to come.
2. Take a shopping list to the store with you.
3. Plan the time to do the prep work.

Regarding coffee, I suggest what a friend of mine did when doing this Cleanse. Move your coffee maker out to the garage and replace it with a boxed set of teas. She said it made a big difference in the cues she was seeing and set her up to have tea in the morning very easily.

Dinner for Day 1 calls for a pasta sauce. If you plan to make your own sauce, do it the night before to make Day 1 easier. Look ahead for the recipe. Alternatively, it's perfectly fine to use a store-bought jar of organic pasta sauce. If you do make your sauce in advance, store it in the refrigerator.

Day 1

Breakfast: 12 ounces water

Oatmeal and Fruit

Ingredients: 4 ounces oatmeal, 1 cup water, 1-2 ounces of plain or vanilla soy/rice/coconut/almond/hemp milk, ½ banana sliced and a sprinkle of cinnamon, or 1 ounce of a dried fruit (raisins, apricots, cranberries, blueberries)

Preparation: Bring the water to a boil, stir in the oatmeal, keep at medium-high heat, stirring occasionally until the oatmeal is the consistency you desire. Once the oatmeal is cooked, you can pour 1-2 ounces of plain or vanilla soy/rice/coconut/almond/hemp milk. For flavor options top with ½ banana and a sprinkle of cinnamon; or 1 ounce of a dried fruit (raisins, apricots, cranberries, blueberries).

Enjoy, it's going to be a great day!

1 cup tea optional

The first three days may be the toughest as you will want to grab for the foods your body is used to. Recognize that for what it is and stay strong. If you feel you need to eat something, eat fruit or beans until the next meal. You can also pick a snack from the Snack List at the end of this book.

Lunch: Tabouleh and Barley

Note regarding barley: In this Cleanse, pearl barley is used, but there is a variety of barleys available. Hulled barley, or barley groats, has the bran layer, pearl barley does not. While barley groats are very nutritious, some people have a hard time digesting it. Red barley is available and is very pretty and still nutritious too. For any recipe calling for pearl barley, you can substitute one of the other barleys to try something new. You may like it!

Ingredients, pearl barley: ½ cup pearl barley (you can substitute brown rice), ½ teaspoon olive oil, 1 cup water

Ingredients, tabouleh: ¼ cup green onions chopped, ½ cup parsley chopped, 1/8 cup mint chopped, ¼ cup cherry tomatoes chopped, ½ teaspoon garlic minced, 1/8 cup olive oil, 1/8 cup fresh lemon juice, ½ -1 teaspoon salt, ¼ teaspoon pepper

Personal favorite: I like to dry-roast grains before putting them in the boiling liquid. This cooks off some of the sugars. In a large skillet on high heat, pour the grains in, stir occasionally being careful not to burn them. Once all the grains are a light brown color, remove from the heat. They are ready to be poured into the boiling liquid for the next cooking step.

Cooking the barley: With the stove on high heat, pour the water into the pot, add the olive oil, and bring the water to a boil. Stir in the barley, cover, and simmer for 20-23 minutes, or until the water is absorbed. Cool and refrigerate.

Preparation, tabouleh: In a bowl, place the green onions, parsley, mint, cherry tomatoes, and garlic, drizzle on the olive oil, fresh lemon juice, salt, and pepper, and toss all together. I actually like my tabouleh real lemony so I keep adding lemon juice and tasting until it has just the right amount of zing!

Putting it all together: In a bowl, place 1 cup of cooked barley, or rice, add the tabouleh, and you have a delightful lunch!

Dinner: Polenta in Pasta Sauce

Ingredients, pasta sauce: 2 tablespoons extra-virgin olive oil, 1 cup onions chopped, 4 cloves garlic chopped, 25 ounces chopped tomatoes, 1.6 ounce can tomato paste, 1 teaspoon salt, ¼ teaspoon black pepper, ¼ teaspoon dried oregano, 12 organic fresh basil leaves chopped
Options: ½ - ¾ pound mushrooms chopped, 1 ounce balsamic vinegar, 1-2 ounces baby carrots chopped, pinch of red chili pepper flakes

Ingredients, polenta: 4 cups water, 1½ cup organic polenta. This will make enough for 4-8 people.

Time-Saving Tip: If you would like, buy one 18-ounce tube of organic polenta (buy two tubes of polenta if you are feeding four people), and one 25-ounce jar of organic pasta sauce.

Ingredients for the final product: a drizzle of extra-virgin olive oil, 1 tablespoon minced garlic, ½ diced onion, 1 bulb diced fennel, 8 diced mushrooms

Option to add white cannellini beans if you feel you would need a little more substance/calories. If so, add 14 ounces of cooked cannellini beans. It would be much easier to buy one can of organic cannellini beans. If you are going to be cooking them, wash and drain the beans first. Place them in a big pot, cover with water, bring to a boil, then reduce the heat, cover and simmer for about one hour or until the beans are tender.

Preparation, pasta sauce: Pour the olive oil in a large pot and heat on high, add the onions and garlic, stirring, reduce heat to medium for 10 minutes, and stir about every 2 minutes. Add the chopped tomatoes, tomato paste, salt, pepper, and any of the options you want, and bring to a boil, reduce the heat so the sauce is simmering, and cover. Let simmer for 1-2 hours.

Preparation, polenta: Pour the 4 cups of water in a big pot on high heat and bring to a boil, then reduce to simmer. While stirring, slowly add the polenta. Using a whisk helps prevent it from clumping. Continue stirring the polenta until it has gotten thick and pulls away from the sides of the pan, about 20-50 minutes. Pour the polenta onto a wooden (not plastic) cutting board and shape into a square. Let the polenta cool and settle for a few minutes and then you may cut it into 1-inch thick slices in order to prepare it for the next cooking step.

Putting it all together: In a large skillet, heat on high, drizzle extra-virgin olive oil, sauté 1 tablespoon minced garlic, 2 minutes over medium-high heat. Add ½ diced onion, 1 bulb diced fennel, 8 diced mushrooms, and sauté 8 -10 minutes. Add 25 ounces of the organic pasta sauce you made or bought heat 10 minutes, stirring occasionally. Place the slices of polenta in the skillet, heat each side 8-10 minutes. Once you are heating the polenta on the second side you will then add in the cannellini beans if you are opting for them. Right before serving, sprinkle the fresh basil leaves on top.

Night-Before Prep: Day 2 dinner is black bean chili. If using dried beans, soak them overnight.

Soaking beans is very easy. Pour the measured amount of beans into a large mixing bowl, cover with room temperature or cold water, and leave overnight. That's it, super easy! Before cooking the beans, drain off the soaking water and rinse them.

Time-Saving Tip: If you want to make tomorrow morning easier, cut all the veggies for tomorrow night's dinner tonight.

"I feel good!"

_____
_____
_____
_____
_____
_____
_____
_____
_____

Day 2

Breakfast: 12 ounces water

Toast and Avocado

Ingredients: 2 pieces of wheat free bread (kamut, spelt, multigrain bread, or rye), 1 avocado; and 1 protein smoothie. Choose any smoothie from the smoothie list toward the end of the Cleanse.

Preparation: Toast the bread. Slice the avocado lengthwise, and place the slices on the toast. Make your smoothie.

Enjoy a great breakfast that will supply you with solid nutrients and help you feel ready to get things done!

1 cup tea optional

Lunch: Lettuce Wrap

Ingredients: 1 full leaf iceberg lettuce. Choose as many of these as you would like: 2 ounces shredded carrots, 2 ounces diced cucumbers, 2 ounces diced tomatoes, 2 ounces bean sprouts, 2 ounces edemame beans, 2 ounces of diced bell pepper any color you prefer, 1 ounce diced zucchini. Drizzle either peanut dressing, balsamic vinaigrette, sesame dressing, or spread hummus on the inside leaf before wrapping.

Ingredients Hummus: 15 ounces of cooked chick peas, 1 tablespoon extra virgin olive oil, 1 tablespoon water, 1/3 cup fresh lemon juice, 1 teaspoon salt. You can easily cook the chick peas by boiling them at a hard boil for 3 hours, or buy 1-15 ounce can. If the chick peas are canned, drain and rinse them off.

Time-Saving Tip: Many stores carry hummus in the refrigerator section. If time is a variable that gets short in your life, make this easy and go buy hummus at the store. My personal favorite is Garlic Hummus – Yum! You can eat hummus often throughout this cleanse as it is made from beans and is a very good source of healthy fats. You can snack on hummus as well as use it in meals.

Preparation, hummus: Place all ingredients in a Vitamix® or blender and puree.

There are numerous variations on hummus:

For **garlic hummus**, add 2-3 large cloves of roasted garlic in before blending.

For **roasted red bell pepper hummus**, add ½-1 whole roasted red bell pepper before blending.

For **olive hummus**, add ½ cup pitted olives before blending. With these variations, start with the lower amount of this extra ingredient and taste it before you increase the ingredient. For example, some people prefer a very garlicky flavor while others prefer just a subtle taste of garlic.

Balsamic vinaigrette: ¼ cup balsamic vinegar, ½ cup extra-virgin olive oil, ¼ teaspoon salt, ¼ teaspoon black pepper, 1 clove garlic minced.

Optional: 1 tablespoon Dijon mustard; or 1 teaspoon honey. Whisk all ingredients together. Refrigerate after use. This will hold for two weeks.

Sesame Dressing: 1 tablespoon minced garlic, 1 tablespoon minced ginger, 3- 6 tablespoons Bragg's Liquid Aminos or tamari sauce; try it with 3 tablespoons first, then add more for your taste preference. (Soy sauce is made with wheat, so while you are on the Cleanse substitute soy sauce with either Bragg's Liquid Aminos or tamari sauce.), 1 tablespoon rice wine vinegar, 1 tablespoon sesame oil, ¼ cup vegetable oil
Optional: 2 tablespoons vegan mayonnaise (it will make it creamy)
Optional: ¾ teaspoon red chili pepper flakes
Optional : 1 tablespoon honey
Whisk all ingredients together until they are well blended. Refrigerate after use. This will hold for 2 weeks.

Peanut dressing: ½ cup non-crunchy peanut butter, 2 ½ teaspoons sesame oil, ½ cup vegetable oil, 2 tablespoons tamari sauce, 1 tablespoon rice wine vinegar, 1 lime, 2 cloves of garlic chopped, 3 tablespoons honey, 1 tablespoon ginger chopped, ½ cup cilantro chopped, ¼ teaspoon salt, 3 tablespoons water

Dinner: Black Bean Chili

Ingredients: 2 cups of dried black beans, 2 tablespoons olive oil, 1 medium red bell pepper (orange or yellow work fine too), ¾ cup diced carrots, 3 large celery stalks chopped, 1 medium red onion diced (white or yellow can be substituted), 16 ounces organic vegetable stock, 2 teaspoons salt, 1 teaspoon pepper, 2 teaspoons ground mild red chili. If you like hotter spices, add 1-2 teaspoons of ground hot chili pepper. This makes about 8 servings if using the 2 cups of black beans. You can reduce this if you want less. Keep in mind you can use some of the beans for tomorrow's dinner, which is tacos.
Optional: 3- 6 cloves of garlic diced
If you soaked the beans overnight, drain and rinse them off in a colander, and put to the side.

If you did not soak them, do a quick soak. Place the beans in a pot, cover with water, and bring to a boil. Remove from the heat, but keep covered for 1 hour. Drain and rinse and now they are ready to be cooked.

Time-Saving Tip: If you need to, cut all these veggies up the night before, making your morning easier.

Crock pot preparation: In a crock pot turned to high, pour in the olive oil. After 2 minutes add the bell pepper, carrots, celery, and onion, and garlic (if using), stirring until all the ingredients are blended. Cover and let cook for 1 hour. Then place the beans into the crock pot and pour the vegetable stock over it. Add the seasonings, salt and pepper, and stir until everything is well blended. Cook on high for 4-5 hours or low for 6 hours.

Crock pot Time-Saving Tip: If you need to just put all the ingredients in the crock pot right away in the morning and head out the door, that would still be fine and your chili will still taste very good.

Stove top preparation: heat a stock pot with the extra-virgin olive oil for 1-2 minutes on high, add the bell pepper, carrots, celery, onion, and garlic (if using), stirring the mixture for 7-10 minutes. Pour the beans into the stock pot, and pour the vegetable stock over them. Add the seasonings, salt and pepper, and stir until everything is well blended. Cook on high until it reaches a boil, then reduce to low-medium heat to simmer for 2 ½-3 hours, stirring occasionally.

Serving this over rice, quinoa, or barley would increase the carbohydrates available for your body and may satisfy your appetite even more.

Time-Saving Tip: Prep for tomorrow: Tomorrow's Potato Scramble breakfast takes a little more prep time than usual. If you have time tonight, cook the potatoes and refrigerate them, making sure you remove them from the boiling water before they get too soft or mushy. In the morning, start at the step where you place them in the skillet. Please refer to tomorrow's breakfast for cooking instructions.

"I feel good!"

_____

_____

_____

_____

_____

_____

_____

_____

_____

Day 3

Breakfast: 12 ounces water

Potato Scramble

Ingredients: 6 medium red potatoes, 2 cups water, 1 tablespoon olive oil, ½ teaspoon salt, a sprinkle of pepper. **Options:** 1 ounce soy taco meat or soy chorizo, and 1 ounce fresh parsley chopped, or 1 teaspoon dried parsley flakes. If you are not using either soy product, you can use the parsley on its own or 1 ounce fresh basil chopped, or 1 teaspoon dried basil flakes. The soy product tastes great with parsley, not so much with basil. If you like red chili flakes, this is the perfect dish for that. Or even a hot sauce.

Preparation: Bring 2 cups of water to a boil. Wash the potatoes and cut in quarters, steam on high heat with a lid on for about 20 minutes, or until the potatoes are slightly soft but not fully cooked or mushy. Check every few minutes by sticking a fork in them. As the potatoes are just about finished cooking, turn on a skillet to high and pour in the olive oil. Once the potatoes are slightly soft, remove them from the water and place them in the hot skillet. This would be the time to put the soy product in the skillet also. Stir the potatoes on high heat until they are browned; add in the parsley or basil, and salt and pepper.

Enjoy! A breakfast meant to give you energy to burn!

1 cup tea optional

Lunch: Green Bean Salad

Ingredients: 6 ounces green beans steamed, 2 ounces shredded carrots, sesame or garlic dressing, 1 handful of slivered almonds
Optional: ¾ teaspoon red chili pepper flakes, or 2 tablespoons ground chia seeds, and/or 2 tablespoons ground flax seeds. (If you do not have a food processor, a coffee grinder works great.)

With this meal, if you feel that you would need more substance, definitely add both the chia and flax seeds. You could also add a handful of pecans to this; it would taste very good with all the other ingredients.

Preparation, steaming the green beans: In a medium pot bring 8 ounces of water to a boil. Place the green beans in the pot and cover, steaming on high for 8-10 minutes. It is better to not overcook your vegetables; they should be a little hard.

Sesame Dressing: 1 tablespoon minced garlic, 1 tablespoon minced ginger, 3- 6 tablespoon Bragg's Liquid Aminos or tamari sauce. (Try it with 3 tablespoons first, then add more for your taste preference. Soy sauce is made with wheat so while you are on the Cleanse substitute soy sauce with either Bragg's Liquid Aminos or tamari sauce.) 1 tablespoon rice wine vinegar, 1 tablespoon sesame oil, ¼ cup vegetable oil.
Optional: 2 tablespoons vegan mayonnaise, it will make it creamy
Optional: ¾ teaspoon red chili pepper flakes
Optional: 1 tablespoon honey
Whisk all ingredients together until they are well blended. Refrigerate after use. This will hold for 2 weeks.

Garlic dressing: 6 tablespoon olive oil, ½ lemon juiced, 3 tablespoon of red or white wine vinegar, 3 cloves of garlic minced, ½ -1 teaspoon salt, 1/8 - ½ teaspoon pepper.
Optional: 2 tablespoons tamari sauce or Braggs Liquid Aminos, or ½ - 1 teaspoon oregano
To make this dressing, you can whisk the ingredients or blend them in the blender or the Vitamix®. First, whisk or blend the olive oil, lemon juice, and vinegar until smooth. Then add in the remaining ingredients and whisk or blend until smooth. Refrigerate before using if there is time. Store any leftovers in the refrigerator. You have the option to use garlic dressing on Day 8. This stores for up to 2 weeks.

Putting it all together: In a bowl, layer the green beans and shredded carrots, pour some sesame dressing or garlic dressing on top, and sprinkle with a handful of slivered almonds. Layer on the options, if desired. Enjoy!

Dinner: Taco Taco

Ingredients: 2 Organic corn taco shells, fill with any combination of the following: ¾ cup shredded green or red cabbage, ¾ cup shredded carrots, 1 sliced avocado, 6 ounces Pico de Gallo, ¾ cup corn, ½ cup shredded rice cheese or soy cheese, ½-1 cup black beans, and package of soy taco meat
Option: use black beans from last night's dinner
Option: use guacamole in place of sliced avocados (recipe follows)

Preparation, guacamole: shell 1 ripe avocado, cut into small pieces, and scoop into a bowl. Squeeze ½ or 1 full lemon or lime (lime is tangier) onto the avocado and sprinkle a little salt on it. Using a fork, mash the avocado to desired consistency, chunky or smooth.

Ingredients. Pico de Gallo: ½ pound plum tomatoes, ¼ cup chopped red onion, 1 ounce chopped cilantro, 1 tablespoon lime or lemon juice (lime juice will make it tangier, lemon juice not as tangy but still has a bite to it).

Optional: 1 tablespoon minced and seeded jalapeño peppers; 1 teaspoon to 1 tablespoon minced garlic, as per your taste (even keep out entirely, if you prefer).

In a bowl, combine all ingredients and toss together.

Putting it all together: Place two corn tortillas on a plate, layer on your ingredients, and enjoy!

"I feel good!"

Day 4

Breakfast: 12 ounces water

7-Grain Hot Cereal and Fruit

Bob's Red Mill has a version of this, or you may be able to find this at your local health food store, possibly even in the bin grains. It is highly nutritious and a very clean source of carbohydrates, proteins, fiber, a large variety of phytonutrients, and an excellent way to start your day. It's also a great addition to your regular diet to help lower cholesterol, as well as lower your LDLs and triglycerides. This cereal will provide you with a good amount of necessary fiber and also help stabilize your blood glucose levels, so it is very good for diabetics and those who are developing insulin resistance or metabolic syndrome. Because it is a natural cereal, it may take a little getting used to because it does not have added man-made ingredients. So allow your taste buds to get used to it. Seven-Grain cereal is one of my favorites because of its clean taste.

Ingredients: 4 ounces 7-grain hot cereal, 1 cup water, ½ cup soy/rice/coconut/almond/hemp milk. Pick 1 fruit option: ½ banana sliced; or 1 ounce of fresh raspberries, or blueberries, or 1 ounce of dried fruit, such as raisins, apricots (chop the dried apricots into bite-size pieces), a sprinkle of cinnamon.

Preparation: Bring the water to a boil, stir in the 7-grain cereal, and keep at medium-high heat, stirring occasionally until the water is absorbed. Once the cereal is cooked, pour it into a bowl. You can add ½- 1 ounce of soy/rice/coconut/almond/hemp milk into the cereal, your fruit choice, and sprinkle of cinnamon.

This is a breakfast to allow you to go forth and accomplish!

1 cup tea optional

Lunch: Broccoli Slaw

Ingredients: 2 broccoli stalks shredded, 1 carrot shredded, toss with either the balsamic vinaigrette dressing (recipe below), or sesame dressing (recipe listed on Day 2 and also at the end of the Cleanse) **Options**: ½ chopped red onion; ½ chopped avocado; 1 handful slivered almonds or pine nuts; ¼ cup chopped green onions, 1 ounce grated soy or rice cheese, mozzarella or cheddar; 1 tablespoon chopped parsley

Balsamic vinaigrette: ¼ cup balsamic vinegar, ½ cup extra-virgin olive oil, ¼ teaspoon salt, ¼ teaspoon black pepper, 1 clove garlic minced **Optional**: 1 tablespoon Dijon mustard; or 1 teaspoon honey Whisk all ingredients together.

Preparation, broccoli slaw: In a bowl, place the shredded broccoli and carrots, add in any of the other options. Drizzle on the chosen dressing and toss together. Depending on how many of the options you chose, this may have yielded a large amount. Eat at most 1 ½ cups of the final product. You can either refrigerate the remainder or, even better, share it with a friend.

Dinner: Awesome Nut-Grain Loaf

Ingredients: 1 ½ cups quinoa, 3 cups water, 1 teaspoon olive oil, 14 ounces red beans, 2 tablespoons garlic minced, ¾ cup carrots chopped, ¾ cup celery chopped, ½ - ¾ cup onions minced, ½ cup almonds ground (If you do not have a food processor, a coffee grinder works great.), ½ cup cashews ground, ½ cup pepitas ground, 2 tablespoons tamari, ½ cup tahini, 2 tablespoons fresh lemon juice, salt and pepper to taste (tamari is already a little salty)

This meal does take a bit of time. Once it is in the oven, it takes 50 minutes, and there are a few steps before that. Make this on a night that works with your schedule.

Substitution options: You can substitute the tahini with 2 more tablespoons of lemon juice and ½ cup hummus. You can also replace the pepitas with ½ cup pecans.
This does make quite a bit, especially if you will be the only one eating it. If that is the case, cut the ingredients in half.

Quinoa preparation: Do this step first. In a medium sauce pan, pour the 3 cups of water and 1 teaspoon of olive oil and bring to a boil. Pour in the quinoa, stir, and cover. Bring to a boil, reduce heat to medium, and simmer until the water is absorbed, about 23 minutes. Tomorrow's breakfast is Barley+. If you would like, replace the barley with quinoa and cook an extra 3 ounces now, yielding 6 ounces for breakfast. Of course, add 6 more ounces of water if you are cooking the extra quinoa. If you do want barley with breakfast tomorrow, it would save you time to cook that tonight if you get the chance. While this is cooking, move on to the bean and veggie preparation.

Preheat the oven to 350 degrees

Preparation, red beans: In a large pot, on high heat, place the red beans and cover with water. Cover the pot and bring to a boil, and boil for 1 hour.

Red Beans Time-Saving Tip: To make this meal much easier and faster, you can buy 1 can of red beans, already cooked. All you would have to do is drain and rinse the canned red beans.

Preparing the aromatics: In a skillet, drizzle 1 tablespoon of olive oil and let heat for about 1-2 minutes. Add the garlic, carrots, celery, and onion, and sauté on medium heat for about 7 minutes. Set aside.

Next ground the almonds, cashews, and pepitas. Set aside.

Bringing it all together: In a large mixing bowl, place the quinoa, and add in the red beans and mix together. Next, stir in the aromatic vegetables. Once these are evenly blended, stir in the ground nuts, tamari, tahini, and lemon juice, and salt and pepper to taste. Stir until evenly blended.

Grease a Pyrex cooking pan (approximately 8"x8"x2") or 2 loaf pans, with either olive oil or canola oil margarine. Place the blended mixture into the pan(s) and spread it out evenly. Place in the oven and bake for about 50 minutes. The top should be just slightly browned.

"I feel good!"

_____

_____

_____

_____

_____

_____

_____

_____

_____

Day 5

Breakfast: 12 ounces water

Barley +

Ingredients: 3 ounces uncooked pearl barley (3 ounces uncooked barley will yield 6 ounces of cooked barley), 6 ounces of water, ½ teaspoon olive oil, 1 teaspoon canola margarine. Optional additions for this morning are 1 handful of dried cranberries and 1 handful of pine nuts; or 1 handful of dried pomegranate seeds and 1 handful of diced cashews. This is really great! You could even sprinkle cinnamon or all-spice on this. One more option, and a great way to get your essential fatty acids, is to sprinkle on 2 tablespoons of ground flax seeds, which will give this a nutty flavor.

Personal favorite: I like to dry-roast grains before putting them in the boiling liquid. This cooks off some of the sugars. Pour the grains into a large skillet on high heat, stirring occasionally and making sure not to burn the grains. Once all the grains are a light brown color, remove from the heat, and hold aside until the next cooking step.

Time-Saving Tip: You will be having barley for lunch tomorrow. It would save you time to cook an extra 3 ounces today. If you are cooking the extra, add 6 ounces more of water. Then store the extra 6 ounces of cooked barley in the refrigerator.

Preparation, barley: Pour the water in a pot, pour in ½ teaspoon olive oil, and bring to a boil. Stir in the barley, cover and simmer for 20-23 minutes, or until the water is absorbed.
In a bowl place 6 ounces of hot barley. While the barely is hot, mix in a little canola margarine to moisten. Top off with any of the options you want and enjoy!

You are now energized for the morning!

1 cup tea optional

Lunch: Refreshing Avocado, Fennel, and Tomato Salad

Ingredients: 1 avocado, 1 fennel bulb chopped, ½ cup diced tomatoes (regular, cherry, roma), ¼ cup balsamic vinegar or balsamic vinaigrette dressing (recipe listed on Day 4 and also at the end of the Cleanse)

Preparation: Place all the ingredients in a bowl, dress with your choice of balsamic vinegar or balsamic vinaigrette dressing. Yum!

Dinner: Pasta With Sun-Dried Tomato Pesto

Ingredients, sun-dried tomato pesto: 2 heads of garlic, 12 sun-dried tomato halves, 2 teaspoons fresh oregano, 2 tablespoons organic extra-virgin olive oil, 1 teaspoon red wine vinegar, ¼ teaspoon salt. **Option:** ¼ teaspoon crushed red pepper

Ingredients: 1 bag quinoa pasta, or corn/rice/spinach pasta

Preparation, sun-dried tomato pesto: Pre-heat oven to 400 degrees. Roast 2 heads of garlic by cutting off the first ¼ of each head, wrap in foil, and cook until soft, usually 45 minutes. Soak 12 sun-dried tomato halves, about 2 ounces, in a bowl of boiling water to soften. Cover the bowl. Usually this takes 20 minutes. Keep the water you are soaking the sun-dried tomatoes in, as you will use it later. Place the softened tomatoes in a blender or food processor, add the oregano, organic extra-virgin olive oil, vinegar, and salt, (and crushed red pepper if using this) and 6 ounces of the water the dried tomatoes were soaked in. Add the roasted garlic by squeezing it out of the shell. Pulse on high a few times and then continue blending until it gets to the consistency you want.

Prepare the pasta as directed on the package. Do check the pasta often, some of the wheat-free pastas cook quickly and can get soft fast, and they do not taste good if they are mushy.

Putting it all together: Right after cooking the pasta, drain it, and pour it into a bowl. Ladle on the sun-dried tomato pesto and toss together.

Night-Before Prep Day 6: Soak ½ cup garbanzo beans in water overnight.

Also: You will need either the cilantro dressing or balsamic vinaigrette dressing for tomorrow's lunch; it is easier to have one of these already waiting in the refrigerator for you.

"I feel good!"

_____

_____

_____

_____

_____

_____

_____

_____

_____

_____

Day 6

Breakfast: 12 ounces water

Fruit Salad

Ingredients: ½ banana sliced, 6 strawberries sliced, 1-2 ounces grapes sliced.

Options: replace the grapes with ½ mango sliced; replace the grapes with 1-2 ounces blueberries; replace the grapes with 1-2 ounces raspberries.

Preparation: Place your cut-up fruit in a bowl and stir together just to mix the fruits up.

Even more options: have just 2 of the fruits and 1 piece of toast, either kamut, spelt, rye, or multigrain

Option 3: If you think you will still be hungry with just fruit, then definitely eat 1 piece of toast.

Your day will be bright when you start it with such a bright breakfast!

1 cup tea optional

Lunch: Protein- Packed Grains and Beans

Ingredients, pearl barley: 3 ounces pearl barley, 6 ounces water, ½ teaspoon extra-virgin olive oil

Ingredients, garbanzo beans: 3 ounces garbanzo beans, 3 cups water

Time-Saving Tip: You can buy 1 can of garbanzo beans, and it really would help in this case. It comes down to sticking to the vegan foods. At the end of the day, whether you have bought the already-cooked beans or spent the time cooking them, you will have eaten beans. The goal is to stay on this Full-Body Cleanse, and eating beans will reduce your cholesterol. Beans also add fiber to your diet, helping reduce your risk for colon cancer. The goal is to keep beans a part of your life!

Ingredients for the final dish: 2 ounces diced green onions, 2 ounces diced tomatoes, 2 ounces diced Kalamata olives, and dressing of your choice, either balsamic vinaigrette (listed on Day 2 and at the end of the Cleanse), or cilantro (recipe below).

Cooking the garbanzo beans: If you soaked the beans in water overnight, drain and rinse them. If you did not soak them, do a quick soak. Place the beans in a pot, cover with water, and bring to a boil. Remove from the heat, but keep covered for 1 hour. Drain and rinse and now they are ready to be cooked. Pour 2 cups of cold water in the pot, add the beans, cover, and bring to a boil, keep them covered and reduce to a simmer, cook for 3-4 hours.

Personal favorite: I like to dry-roast grains before putting them in the boiling liquid. This cooks off some of the sugars. Pour the grains into a large skillet on high heat, stirring occasionally and making sure not to burn the grains. Once all the grains are a light brown color, remove from the heat, and hold aside until the next cooking step.

Cooking the barley: Pour the water in a pot, add ½ teaspoon olive oil, and bring to a boil. Stir in the barley, cover and simmer for 20-23 minutes, or until the water is absorbed.

Ingredients, cilantro dressing: 3 cloves of garlic chopped, 1 cup cilantro packed and chopped, ¾ cups parsley packed and chopped, 1 tablespoon fresh ginger minced, ¾ cup fresh lime juice, 1 tablespoon wine vinegar or apple cider vinegar, ¾ cup extra-virgin olive oil, ¼-½ teaspoon salt, ¼ teaspoon pepper **Optional**: ½ -1 tablespoon honey (I prefer no sweetener at all, so decide for yourself); 1 pinch of red chili pepper flakes.

Preparation, cilantro dressing: In the food processor or the Vitamix®, turn on and add in the garlic, cilantro, parsley, and ginger. Process until all are finely chopped. Keeping the food processor or the Vitamix® on, add the lime juice, vinegar, olive oil, salt, pepper, and any of the options you want. Process until all have become a smooth creamy dressing. Refrigerate any unused portion. You will be using this with lunch on Day 8.

Putting it all together: Put the ¾ cup cooked barley in a bowl, add the garbanzo beans, green onions, tomatoes, Kalamata olives, dress with cilantro dressing, and you have a great meal!
Fruit is a great midday snack to fuel your brain and all your cells!

Dinner: **Roasted Vegetables** One of my absolute favorites!

Pre-heat oven to 325 degrees.

Ingredients, vegetables: 4 zucchini sliced in quarters lengthwise, 2-4 onions quartered, 2-4 bell-peppers (any color) quartered (or leave whole and refer below for details on bell peppers), ½-1 full bunch asparagus cut into thirds, 1-3 bulbs fennel cut in half
Options: add or use these as replacements to any of the above listed vegetables: 4 yellow squash; 4-6 carrots; 4-6 parsnips; 2-4 beets; ½-1 cup Brussels sprouts; 1 small eggplant; 3 Japanese eggplants; 10-15 radishes

Ingredients, hummus: 15 ounces of cooked chick peas, 1 tablespoon extra-virgin olive oil, 1 tablespoon water, 1/3 cup fresh lemon juice, 1 teaspoon salt. You can easily cook the chick peas by boiling them at a hard boil for 3 hours, or buy one 15-ounce can. If the chick peas are canned, rinse them off.

Hummus Time-Saving Tip: Many stores carry hummus in the refrigerator section. If time is a variable that gets short in your life, make this easy and go buy hummus at the store. My personal favorite is Garlic Hummus – Yum! You can eat hummus often throughout this cleanse as it is made from beans and is a very good source of healthy fats. You can snack on hummus as well as use it in meals.

Ingredients, olive tapenade: ¾ cup Kalamata olives, ¾ cup black olives, ¾ cup green olives, 1-2 tablespoons capers drained, 1-2 cloves garlic, ½ tablespoon flat leaf parsley, ½ tablespoon basil, ¼ tablespoon oregano, ½ teaspoon lemon juice, ¼ cup extra-virgin olive oil
Option: red chili flakes

Olive tapenade Time-Saving Tip: Olive tapenade is something I definitely prefer to buy (I love the one I make, but it takes time). I like a blend of black and green olive tapenade. But if you would really like to make your own, I've provided my recipe, below.

Other Ingredients for the final meal: 2 slices wheat-free flat bread or 2 wheat-free pita pockets

Preparation, vegetables: Roast the bell peppers whole and then once they are done, place them in a brown paper bag, let cool, then peel away the skin. You can leave the skin on, but it has a slightly bitter taste. Slit the bell peppers in half and remove the seeds and discard them. Cut them into bite-size pieces.
Place all the cut vegetables in a roasting pan, along with the bell peppers, and drizzle with extra-virgin olive oil, a sprinkle of salt and pepper, and a drizzle of balsamic vinegar. Cook for 1 hour, mixing every 15 minutes. Cook to desired taste. For softer veggies, cook longer.

Preparation, hummus: Place all ingredients in a Vitamix® or blender and puree.
There are numerous variations on hummus:
For **garlic hummus**, add 2-3 large cloves of roasted garlic in before blending.
For **roasted red bell pepper hummus**, add ½-1 whole roasted red bell pepper before blending.
For **olive hummus**, add ½ cup pitted olives before blending. With these variations, start with the lower amount of this extra ingredient and taste it before you increase the ingredient. For example, some people prefer a very garlicky flavor while others prefer just a subtle taste of garlic.

Preparation, olive tapenade: Place all of the ingredients into a food processor or the Vitamix®. Pulse several times until your tapenade reaches your desired consistency. Some people like their tapenades chunky and others prefer more of a paste. This will hold for up to 2 weeks in the refrigerator.

There are ways to vary tapenade to make it perfect for your own taste: you could use only Kalamata olives, omitting any green or black olives, which would give it a milder flavor. Kalamata olives are the classic olive for this dish. Another option is to use only green olives and Kalamata olives. For a less salty version, use only black olives and Kalamata olives, as black olives are not as salty as green. You can leave out Kalamata olives and use just black and green olives. You could also play with the amount of garlic, lemon juice, and capers.

Putting it all together: Bring the wheat-free flat bread or wheat-free pita pockets, hummus, olive tapenade, and the roasted veggies to the table and enjoy all combinations of these items. Try putting hummus on the bread and then adding some roasted veggies; or just the veggies on the bread; or the tapenade on the bread and roasted veggies on top. This is a great dinner to enjoy with friends!

Night-Before Prep for Dinner Day 7: While your veggies are roasting, you can make use of this time to prep for tomorrow's dinner. If you would like, cut the veggies you will be using in your split pea soup.

"I feel good!"

_____

_____

_____

_____

_____

_____

_____

_____

_____

Day 7

Breakfast: 12 ounces water

Toast, Hummus, Smoothie (THS)
This is much healthier than the old fashioned BLT!

Ingredients: 2 pieces of wheat-free bread (kamut, spelt, rye, multigrain), 2 ounces hummus, 1 protein smoothie of your choice (all smoothie recipes are written at the end)

Hummus: 15 ounces of cooked chick peas, 1 tablespoon extra-virgin olive oil, 1 tablespoon water, 1/3 cup fresh lemon juice, 1 teaspoon salt. You can easily cook the chick peas by boiling them at a hard boil for 3 hours, or buy one- 15 ounce can. If the chick peas are canned, rinse them off.

Hummus Time-Saving Tip: Many stores carry hummus in the refrigerator section. If time is a variable that gets short in your life, make this easy and go buy hummus at the store. My personal favorite is garlic hummus – Yum! You can eat hummus often throughout this cleanse as it is made from beans and is a very good source of healthy fats. You can snack on hummus as well as use it in meals.

Preparation, hummus: Place all ingredients in a Vitamix® or blender and puree.
There are numerous variations on hummus:
For **garlic hummus**, add 2-3 large cloves of roasted garlic in before blending.
For **roasted red bell pepper hummus**, add ½-1 whole roasted red bell pepper before blending.
For **olive hummus**, add ½ cup pitted olives before blending.

With these variations, start with the lower amount of this extra ingredient and taste it before you increase the ingredient. For example, some people prefer a very garlicky flavor while others prefer just a subtle taste of garlic.

Putting it all together: Toast the bread then spread the hummus on top. Make whichever protein smoothie you would like.

Fueling your body and brain! Enjoy your day!

1 cup tea optional

Lunch: Grains and Celery Stalks With Hummus

Ingredients: 2 celery stalks, 2-4 ounces hummus, 2 ounces diced black olives, 1 cup water, ½ teaspoon extra-virgin olive oil, and ½ cup of any grain you prefer (brown rice, quinoa, millet, barley, or amaranth)

Personal favorite: I like to dry-roast grains before putting them in the boiling liquid. This cooks off some of the sugars. Pour the grains into a large skillet on high heat, stirring occasionally and making sure not to burn the grains. Once all the grains are a light brown color, remove from the heat, and hold aside until the next cooking step.

Preparation: Put the water in a pot, drizzle in ½ teaspoon extra-virgin olive oil, and bring to a boil. Pour in ½ cup of your chosen grain, reduce heat to low, and simmer for 20-23 minutes covered.

For the hummus recipe please refer to today's breakfast.

Putting it all together: Wash 2 celery stalks and fill the center with hummus, and then top with diced black olives. Enjoy your 1 cup of cooked grains with a little Bragg's Liquid Aminos or tamari sauce.

Dinner: Split Pea Soup

Ingredients: 8 ounces of dried split peas, 1 tablespoon extra-virgin olive oil, 1 tablespoon garlic minced, ¼ cup carrots diced, ¼ cup celery diced, ¼ cup red onion diced, ½ teaspoon salt, and ¼ teaspoon pepper. This is a favorite for many people and their families, so they doubled the recipe.

Preparation: In a crock pot, drizzle in the olive oil and layer on the garlic, carrots, celery, and onion. Mix to coat everything with the olive oil. Let this cook on high for 1 hour. After 1 hour, pour the split peas in, sprinkle on the salt and pepper, and cover with either 2 ½ cups of vegetable broth or water (vegetable broth will add more flavor). Cook on high for 3 hours or on low for 5 hours.

Time-Saving Tip: If you need to put all the ingredients in the crock pot at the same time, that would still be fine and your split pea soup will still taste awesome!

Options: Try adding either 1 red, orange, or yellow diced bell pepper in with the other veggies. Try flavoring with white pepper instead of black. For a more robust meal, pair it with some barley or quinoa. Please refer to previous days for cooking instructions for the grain of your choice. Once the grains and split pea soup are fully cooked, place the grains in a bowl and ladle the split pea soup over it.

Tomorrow's Prep: If you need to pack a lunch for work, either roast the veggies for tomorrow's lunch tonight, or you can even have all of them raw. It also might be easier to cut up and then even wrap up the ingredients for tomorrow's lunch tonight. Tomorrow's lunch also calls for cilantro dressing. Take a look ahead and make a plan.

"I feel good!"

_____

_____

_____

_____

_____

_____

_____

_____

_____

Day 8

Breakfast: 12 ounces water

Yogurt and Fruit

Ingredients: Yogurt options: soy or almond yogurt, any flavor you want. Fruit options: pick any 2 fresh fruits form this list: ½ banana sliced, ½ pear sliced, ½ apple sliced, 10 grapes sliced, 8 strawberries sliced, 15 blueberries, 15 raspberries
Pour the yogurt into a bowl, top with the 2 fruits of your choice and enjoy!

A breakfast with a purpose!

1 cup tea optional

Lunch: Arugula and Corn Salad This is very simple and so yummy!

Ingredients: 2 cups arugula, 8 ounces roasted corn, ½ red onion roasted (you can leave the corn and red onion raw, either way is delicious), ½ avocado diced, 2 ounces chopped cashews, 1 tablespoon ground flax or chia seeds, cilantro dressing (recipe on Day 6 and listed at the end).

Preparation: On a cookie sheet, place the cob of fresh corn and red onion and drizzle with olive oil. Place under the broiler on high for 7 minutes, then check. When slightly charred, rotate. Check every 5 minutes, and rotate so that all sides of the corn and onion get slightly charred. Once cooled, cut the corn off the cob, and dice the onion.

Time Saving Option: If you need to pack this up for work, either roast the veggies the day before, or you can even have all of them raw.

Putting it all together: In a bowl, layer the arugula first, then the corn, next the red onion and diced avocado, and sprinkle with the chopped cashews and ground flax or chia seeds. Toss with cilantro dressing.

Option: If you don't like the flavor of cilantro, replace with the balsamic vinaigrette dressing or sesame dressing (both recipes on Day 2 and listed at the end).

Dinner: Roasted Eggplant Salad

Ingredients: 1 medium-large eggplant in slices (if you want to use Japanese eggplants, use 4-6), 3 zucchini sliced in half lengthwise, 2 whole red bell peppers, 2 large carrots peeled and sliced lengthwise, 1 tablespoon salt, 2 tablespoons sesame oil, 1 cucumber diced, 1-2 ounces parsley diced, 1-2 ounces green onions diced, 1-2 ounces cilantro diced, 1-2 ounces cherry tomatoes or sugar plum tomatoes cut in halves, ¼ cup sesame seeds, garlic dressing (recipe on Day 3 and listed at the end).
Option: red chili pepper flakes
Option: substitute peanut dressing (recipe on Day 2 and listed at the end)

Preparation: You may slice the eggplant either to make round slices, or longitudinally for lengthwise pieces. The pieces should be approximately ½ inch thick for easy grilling. Place the sliced eggplant and zucchini on a cookie sheet, and sprinkle with salt to "sweat out" the water, allowing for shorter broiling time. Once you see numerous water drops on the veggies, they're ready to go under the broiler.

In the meantime, drizzle 1 tablespoon of the sesame oil on the bell peppers and carrots and broil on high, for about 7 minutes. Turn when they are slightly charred, and repeat on other side. Char all sides of the bell peppers. Once the bell peppers are done, place them in a brown paper bag and let cool. With the broiler still on high, place the eggplant and zucchini under the broiler and broil for about 7-10 minutes. Once they are slightly charred, flip the pieces over and broil the other side until slightly charred. Let cool and then cut into bite-size pieces. Set aside.

While broiling the eggplant and zucchini, and once the bell peppers have cooled, remove them from the bag, and begin to peel away the skin. This is the easiest way to remove the skin. You can leave the skin on, but it has a bit of a bitter taste and most people prefer the skin removed. Slit the bell peppers in half and remove and discard the seeds, and cut the peppers into bite-size pieces. Set aside.

Make the garlic dressing if you don't have any from the other day.

Dice the cucumber, the parsley, the green onions, cilantro, and the tomatoes, placing in a large bowl and set aside. Once ready, add the eggplant, zucchini, bell peppers, and carrots, sprinkle on the sesame seeds, pour the garlic dressing over, and toss, enjoy! Add in the red chili pepper flakes if desired.

"I feel good!"

_____

_____

_____

_____

_____

_____

_____

_____

_____

Day 9

Breakfast: 12 ounces water

Quesadilla

Ingredients: 2 corn tortillas, 2 ounces shredded soy, rice, or vegan cheese, either American, mozzarella, or cheddar flavored, and 1 avocado sliced. Toppings include your choice of 1 bell pepper of any color chopped; 1 ounce red onion diced; 1 medium tomato chopped, or salsa; 1 ounce jicama chopped.

Preparation: Put the 2 corn tortillas on a broiler pan. Spread the topping you've chosen on to each tortilla then layer on the shredded cheese. Under the broiler, on high, cook the quesadillas until the cheese has melted, about 2-4 minutes. Top with the sliced avocado. Yummy!

This is the best way to begin your day, by making great choices!

1 cup tea optional

Lunch: Multigrain Sandwich

Ingredients: 2 piece of wheat-free bread (kamut, spelt, rye, or multigrain), 1 avocado sliced, 3 ounces sprouts, ¼ cup shredded carrots, 1 slice large tomato, balsamic vinaigrette dressing (listed on Day 2 and also at the end of the Cleanse).

Preparation: Toast the bread, then layer with the sliced avocado, sprouts, shredded carrots, and tomato. Drizzle balsamic vinaigrette dressing on top of the vegetables.

Dinner: Roasted Potatoes and Purple Cabbage

Ingredients: 1 medium-large head of purple cabbage chopped, 12 red potatoes cut, 1 ounce extra-virgin olive oil, 1 ounce balsamic vinegar or 1 ounce Braggs Liquid Aminos, salt, pepper

Preparation: Preheat oven to 325 degrees, cut the cabbage into pieces a little bigger than bite-size. In a big roasting pan place the cabbage, drizzle on the olive oil, and either the balsamic vinegar or Braggs Liquid Aminos and toss together. Cook for 1 hour. While cooking, cut the potatoes into halves. After the cabbage has cooked for 1 hour, remove from the oven and add the potatoes, salt, and pepper, and from this point cook for 1 more hour.

"I feel good!"

_____

_____

_____

_____

_____

_____

_____

_____

_____

Day 10

Day 11 you will need a baked apple with breakfast. Either bake the apple today or tonight so it is ready for you in the morning for breakfast.

Preparation, baked apple: Preheat oven to 350 degrees, wrap the apple in foil, and bake for 40 minutes, store in the refrigerator. A red or green apple is fine. Organic apples are best. You can bake a few apples and store them to eat over the next 3-5 days. Baked apples also make nice snacks or even desserts.

Breakfast: 12 ounces water

Power Toast

Ingredients: 2 pieces of wheat-free bread (kamut, spelt, rye, or multigrain), 2 teaspoon peanut butter, 1 banana sliced, protein smoothie of your choice (protein smoothies are listed at the end).

Preparation: Toast the 2 pieces of bread, spread on the peanut butter and place banana slices on each piece. Make the protein smoothie of your choice, using recipe at the end of the Cleanse.

"Energy and persistence conquer all things"- Benjamin Franklin

1 cup tea optional

Lunch: Cabbage-Wrap

Ingredients: 2 green cabbage leaves, ½ cup diced jicama, ½ cup diced pineapple, ½ cup peeled and shredded carrots, 1 handful chopped almonds, peanut dressing (recipe below)

Options: replace the almonds with cashews; replace the cabbage with butter lettuce, or iceberg lettuce. Replace the peanut dressing with the sesame or balsamic vinaigrette dressing from earlier.

Ingredients, peanut dressing: ½ cup noncrunchy peanut butter, 2 ½ teaspoons sesame oil, ½ cup vegetable oil, 2 tablespoons tamari sauce or Bragg's Liquid Aminos, 1 tablespoon rice wine vinegar, 1 lime juiced, 2 cloves of garlic diced, 3 tablespoons honey, 1 tablespoon ginger diced, ½ cup cilantro chopped, ¼ teaspoon salt, 3 tablespoons water.

Option: add 2-3 teaspoons of crushed red pepper

Preparation, peanut dressing: Place all ingredients in a blender or the Vitamix® and puree until creamy. Refrigerate after use. This will hold for 2 weeks.

Putting it all together: Wash the cabbage leaves and place to the side. Combine the jicama, pineapple, carrots, and almonds in a bowl and mix together with a spoon. Drizzle on a little of the dressing and toss. Divide the mixture in half, scooping one half into each cabbage leaf. Roll this up and enjoy!

This is easy to take to work. Just blend all the vegetable ingredients as directed, and place in one container. Place the 2 cabbage leaves in a plastic bag. Assemble the wrap at lunch time.

Dinner: Quinoa, Butternut Squash, and Spinach

Ingredients, butternut squash: 1 cup cubed butternut squash, 2½ tablespoons sesame oil

Time-Saving Tip: If you buy a medium-large butternut squash, sauté the whole thing tonight. You will have enough left over to eat with dinner on Day 13. This sautéed butternut squash goes perfectly with the dinner planned for that night.

Ingredients, quinoa: 1 cup quinoa or tri-colored quinoa if you can find it (it makes for a prettier dish), 2 cups water, 1 teaspoon sesame oil
Option: replace the quinoa with millet, amaranth, or barley

Ingredients, spinach: 2 cups chopped spinach

Ingredients, sesame dressing: 1 tablespoon minced garlic, 1 tablespoon minced ginger, 3- 6 tablespoons Bragg's Liquid Aminos or tamari sauce (try it with 3 tablespoons first, then add more for your taste preference. Soy sauce is made with wheat, so while you are on the Cleanse substitute soy sauce with either Bragg's Liquid Aminos or tamari sauce.), 1 tablespoon rice wine vinegar, 1 tablespoon sesame oil, ¼ cup vegetable oil
Optional:- 2tablespoons vegan mayonnaise, which will make it creamy
Optional: ¾ teaspoon red chili pepper flakes
Optional: 1 tablespoon honey

Preparation, sesame dressing: Whisk all ingredients together until they are well blended. Refrigerate after use. This will hold for 2 weeks.

Other Ingredients: a sprinkle of pine-nuts or walnuts.

Preparation, butternut squash: Peel 1 butternut squash and cut in half, scoop out the seeds and discard them, cut the squash into cubes. In a large skillet, pour 2 ½ tablespoons sesame oil, and heat on high for about 1 minute. Add the butternut squash and sauté, reduce heat to medium, stir occasionally, and cover. Cook until the butternut squash is tender, about 40 minutes. You will only need 1 cup of this butternut squash tonight. If you made a whole squash, store the remainder in the refrigerator until Day 13 dinner.

Personal favorite: I like to dry-roast grains before putting them in the boiling liquid. This cooks off some of the sugars. In a large skillet on high heat, pour the grains in, stir occasionally being careful not to burn them. Once all the grains are a light brown color, remove from the heat. They are ready to be poured into the boiling liquid for the next cooking step.

Preparation, quinoa: In a pot, pour in the 2 cups of water and the sesame oil and bring to a boil. Stir in the quinoa and return to a boil, reduce heat to low, simmer covered for 15-23 minutes, or until the water is absorbed.

Preparation, spinach: Wash 2 cups of spinach. Chop to small pieces, set aside.

Putting it all together: Place 1 cup of the butternut squash in a large bowl and add the quinoa and spinach. Pour on some of the dressing, depending on whether you doubled the recipe or not. Toss this all together. Once the meal is portioned out, sprinkle the individual servings with either pine-nuts or walnuts.

"I feel good!"

_____
_____
_____
_____
_____
_____
_____
_____
_____

Day 11

Breakfast: 12 ounces water

7-Grain Hot Cereal With Baked Apple and Cinnamon

Ingredients: 4 ounces of 7-grain hot cereal, 1 cup water, 1 baked apple chopped, sprinkle of cinnamon

Preparation, baked apple: Preheat oven to 350 degrees, wrap the apple in foil, and bake for 40 minutes. A red or green apple is fine. Organic apples are best.

Putting it all together: Bring water to a boil. While stirring, add the 7-grain cereal, bring to a boil, and then reduce to simmer. When almost all the water is absorbed, add the chopped baked apple, stirring. Cook until all the water is absorbed or until desired thickness. Once the cereal is cooked, you can pour on 1 ounce of soy, rice, coconut, almond, or hemp milk. Add a sprinkle of cinnamon, and you have a super breakfast!

You are being a great role model, for yourself and your family!

1 cup tea optional

Lunch: Barley Vegetable Salad

Ingredients, pearl barley: ½ cup uncooked pearl barley (will make 1 cup of cooked), 1 cup water or organic vegetable broth. This lunch calls for 1 cup of cooked barley.

Time-Saving Tip: Day 13 dinner is the Ultimate Nut and Grain Burger. You can cook an extra ½ cup of barley here to store and use in 2 nights. I usually double the Ultimate Nut and Grain Burger recipe, making extra for lunch and another dinner. To do so, cook an extra 1 cup of barley today. This means you would be cooking 1 ½ cups of barley now, yielding 1 cup of cooked barley for this lunch, and 2 cups for Day 13 dinner.

Ingredients, vegetables: options are any 4 of the following: 1 ounce diced green or black olives; 1 ounce diced carrots; 1 ounce diced tomatoes; 1 ounce roasted pine nuts; 1 ounce diced steamed green or yellow zucchini (if you like it raw then have it raw); 1 ounce chopped spinach; 1 ounce diced green onions; 1 ounce diced almonds; 1 ounce diced bell peppers, any color; 1 ounce diced steamed broccoli (if you like it raw then have it raw. Also, there is an option to have steamed broccoli with tomorrow's lunch, so steam ½ cup more today); 1 ounce diced celery. Drizzle with 1-2 ounces of sesame dressing, balsamic vinaigrette, or peanut dressing (all recipes listed earlier and at the end of the Cleanse).

Personal favorite: I like to dry-roast grains before putting them in the boiling liquid. This cooks off some of the sugars. In a large skillet on high heat, pour the grains in, stir occasionally being careful not to burn them. Once all the grains are a light brown color, remove from the heat. They are ready to be poured into the boiling liquid for the next cooking step.

Preparation, grains: Put the water or vegetable broth in a pot, drizzle in 1 teaspoon extra-virgin olive oil, and bring to a boil. Pour in the barley and bring to a boil again, then reduce heat to low and simmer for 20-23 minutes covered, or until all the water is absorbed. Use 1 cup of barley for this lunch and store any extra in the refrigerator.

Steaming the vegetables: If you are having green or yellow zucchini or broccoli pour 2 ounces of water into a pot and bring to a boil. Once boiling, place the cut-up vegetables into the pot, cover, and steam for 3-5 minutes. It's best to keep them crunchy – cooked just enough so that digesting them is easy but not overcooked so as to lose all the nutrients.

Putting it all together: In a bowl, place 1 cup cooked barley, the 4 options you chose, and drizzle the dressing of your choice on top and enjoy!

Dinner: Classic Vegetable Soup

Ingredients: 2 tablespoons extra-virgin olive oil, 2 cloves of garlic diced, 3 large celery stalks chopped, 3 big carrots peeled and chopped, 1 red onion chopped, 5 leeks chopped, 3 quarts of water, 6 ounces green beans chopped, 4 ounces turnips chopped, ½ pound potatoes chopped, 2 bay leaves, 2 teaspoons salt, and 1 teaspoon pepper

Preparation: In a large stock pot, pour in the olive oil and heat on high 1-2 minutes. Add the garlic, celery, carrots, red onion, and leeks, lowering the heat to medium-high, and brown for 7-10 minutes, stirring the whole time. Pour in the water, increase to high, and bring to a boil. Once boiling, add the green beans, turnips, potatoes, bay leaves, salt, and pepper, and return to a boil. Once the soup is boiling, reduce the heat to low, and simmer for about 1 ½ hours.

This can be made in a crock pot. Start by pouring in the olive oil, then adding the garlic, celery, carrots, red onion, and leeks. Mix to cover them all with the olive oil. Let these cook for 1 hour. Then add in the water, green beans, turnips, potatoes, bay leaves, salt, and pepper and cook on high for 4 hours or on low for 6 hours. If time is a problem, you can place all of the ingredients into the crock pot at once and head out the door. The flavors will blend together beautifully and you will come home to a yummy dinner to nurture your soul.

Prep for Day 12 lunch: Since tonight's dinner is easy and will be cooking for a while, this is the perfect opportunity to bake the potato you will need for tomorrow's lunch. Preheat the oven to 425 degrees, wash the potato, poke holes on all sides with a fork, wrap it in aluminum foil, and bake for about 1 hour. Remove from oven and let cool. Place this in the refrigerator overnight.

Prep for Day 12 dinner: Dinner tomorrow calls for a pasta sauce. If you plan on making your own pasta sauce, you might want to make it tonight. The recipe is listed with Day 12. Or, you can buy an organic pasta sauce to save time.

"I feel good!"

_____

_____

_____

_____

_____

_____

_____

_____

Day 12

Breakfast: 12 ounces water

Congee
When cooking grains, if you add more liquid and cook them longer than what the usual recipe calls for, you end up making what is called "congee" in Chinese medicine. Congee is very nurturing for your immune system and the spleen.

Ingredients: 3 ounces brown or white rice, 6 ounces water, 3 ounces of either plain or vanilla rice/ coconut/ almond/soy/hemp milk, 1 handful dried apricots chopped, 1 handful dried cranberries chopped, 1 teaspoon all-spice or cinnamon

Preparation: Bring the water to a boil and pour in the rice, bring to a boil, reduce the heat to low, and cook according to package directions for time. After cooking the required time, keep the rice on low heat and add the 3 ounces of plain or vanilla milk, stirring in, and then letting it cook until absorbed. When fully absorbed, pour in a bowl, add the dried apricots, and cranberries, and sprinkle with either all-spice or cinnamon. Enjoy! This is yummy!

Go forth knowing you have been nurtured deeply today!

1 cup tea optional

Lunch: Stuffed Baked Potato

Ingredients: 1 medium potato and whichever options you want from the following: ¼ cup red onion diced; ¼ cup green onion diced; ½ cup steamed broccoli; ½ cup carrots shredded; ¼ cup soy, rice, or almond cheese; 1 tablespoon canola oil margarine; salt and pepper. It is an old bodybuilder's trick to put just salsa or Pico de Gallo on their baked potatoes, as it is fat-free and adds really good flavor.

Preparation: Preheat the oven to 425 degrees. Wash the potato and poke holes on all sides with a fork. Wrap the potato in aluminum foil and place in the oven for about 1 hour.

Prepare any of the above chosen options. Dice the red or green onions if having these.

Steam the broccoli by placing it in just a little boiling water, for about 5 minutes so that the broccoli stays crunchy and retains most of its nutrients. If you prefer, keep the broccoli raw.

Shred the carrots if having carrots.

Shred the dairy-free cheese if you are having it.

For salsa, you can either prepare fresh or buy an already made salsa.

Preparation, salsa/Pico de Gallo: ½ pound plum tomatoes, ¼ cup chopped red onion, 1 ounce chopped cilantro , 1 tablespoon lime or lemon juice (Lime juice will make it tangier, lemon juice not as tangy but still has bite to it.)

Options: 1 tablespoon minced and seeded jalapeño peppers; 1 teaspoon to 1 tablespoon minced garlic (to your taste, or even keep out entirely). In a bowl, combine all ingredients and toss together.

Putting it all together: Place the baked potato in a bowl and cut lengthwise. Add in the options you want and enjoy!

Dinner: Greens in Red Sauce

Ingredients, pasta sauce: 2 tablespoons extra-virgin olive oil, 1 cup onions chopped, 4 cloves garlic chopped, 25 ounces chopped tomatoes, 1.6-ounce can tomato paste, 1 teaspoon salt, ¼ teaspoon black pepper, ¼ teaspoon dried oregano, 12 organic fresh basil leaves diced
Options: ½ - ¾ pounds mushrooms chopped; 1 ounce balsamic vinegar, 1-2 ounces baby carrots chopped, pinch of red chili pepper flakes.
Time-Saving Option: Buy 1 jar of organic pasta sauce, such as basil garlic or chunky tomato, just not a cheese-tomato sauce

Ingredients, greens: 1-2 bundles of kale or collard greens washed and chopped, 4-6 medium red potatoes chopped (red potatoes are best, but you could use 2 medium-sized regular brown potatoes), 1-2 tablespoons olive oil

Preparing the pasta sauce: Pour the olive oil into a large pot heat on high heat, add the onions and garlic, and stir. Reduce heat to medium for 10 minutes and stir about every 2 minutes. Add the tomatoes, tomato paste, salt, black pepper, oregano, and any of the options you want, and bring to a boil. Reduce the heat to a simmer, and leave on for 1-2 hours.

Putting it all together: Pour the olive oil in a crock pot. Layer the cut potatoes on the bottom, and then layer either the kale or collard greens over the potatoes. Cover with the pasta sauce and cook on low for 6 hours, or high for 4 hours. Right before serving sprinkle the basil leaves on top.

Stove-top preparation: This is the same as for a crock pot, but would be cooked on low heat covered for 2-3 hours. Right before serving this dish sprinkle the basil leaves on top.

Night-Before Prep: Tomorrow's breakfast is muesli. It might be easier to make this tonight before the morning.

"I feel good!"

_____

_____

_____

_____

_____

_____

Day 13

Breakfast: 12 ounces water

Muesli

Ingredients: 2 cups rolled oats, ½ cup barley flakes, 1 teaspoon canola oil margarine, ½ cup sunflower seeds, ¼ cup pumpkin seeds, ¼ cup pecans finely chopped, ¼ cup almonds finely chopped, ½ cup wheat germ, 2 tablespoons chia seeds, ½ cup shredded coconut, and ½ cup each of any 2 dried fruits diced, such as raisins, cranberries, apricots, blueberries, apples, pineapple, or mango

Preparation: Preheat the oven to 325 degrees. In a large mixing bowl combine the rolled oats and the barley flakes, mixing evenly. On a baking sheet, very lightly covered with canola oil margarine, spread the oat and barley mixture. Bake for 5 minutes, mixing it halfway through. Mix in the sunflower seeds, pumpkin seeds, pecans, and almonds, blending evenly. Return this to the oven for 5 more minutes, mixing halfway through. Remove from the oven and let cool. Mix in the wheat germ, chia seeds, coconut, and 2 dried fruits. Store this in an air-tight container.

This might become one of your favorite cereals to have around. It's a favorite in our house and we always have some stored. It is a great alternative to store-bought cereals with sweeteners that you really don't need.

You can enjoy this muesli as a hot cereal or cold cereal.

Preparation, hot cereal: Bring 1 cup of water to a boil, stir in 6 ounces of muesli and reduce heat to medium. Continue stirring, this will cook fast. Once the water is absorbed, it is done. You can sprinkle cinnamon or all-spice on top if you would like. This is really yummy!

Preparation, cold cereal: Place 6 ounces of muesli in a bowl and cover with a soy/rice/coconut/almond/hemp milk.

Granola as an option: If you are having a store-bought granola instead, keep in mind that most granolas do have a high amount of sugar, even though it is natural. Pour in your milk of choice. If the milk you are using is not unsweetened, its addition to the granola will add to the sugar content of this breakfast.

There is strength within every time you choose to take care of yourself! Continue building on that strength as you move forward!

1 cup tea optional

Lunch: Hummus Cucumber Sandwich

Ingredients: 2 pieces of wheat-free bread (kamut, spelt, rye, or multigrain), 1-2 ounces hummus, 2 organic Persian cucumbers sliced, or you can substitute with ¾ regular cucumber cut into slices

Hummus: 15 ounces of cooked chick peas, 1 tablespoon extra-virgin olive oil, 1 tablespoon water, 1/3 cup fresh lemon juice, 1 teaspoon salt. You can easily cook the chick peas by boiling them at a hard boil for 3 hours, or buy one 15-ounce can. If the chick peas are canned, drain and rinse them off.

Hummus Time-Saving Tip: Many stores carry hummus in the refrigerator section. If time is a variable that gets short in your life, make this easy and go buy hummus at the store. My personal favorite is garlic hummus – Yum! You can eat hummus often throughout this cleanse as it is made from beans and is a very good source of healthy fats. You can snack on hummus as well as use it in meals.

Preparation, hummus: Place all ingredients in a Vitamix® or blender and puree.

There are numerous variations on hummus:

For **garlic hummus**, add 2-3 large cloves of roasted garlic in before blending.

For **roasted red bell pepper hummus**, add ½-1 whole roasted red bell pepper before blending.

For **olive hummus**, add ½ cup pitted olives before blending. With these variations, start with the lower amount of this extra ingredient and taste it before you increase the ingredient. For example, some people prefer a very garlicky flavor while others prefer just a subtle taste of garlic.

Putting it all together: Toast the bread, layer on the hummus, then the cucumber slices.

Dinner: Ultimate Nut, Grain Burger

This is so tasty, and another of my favorites!

Ingredients: ½ cup uncooked pearl barley (yielding 1 cup cooked barley), 1 cup water, ½ cup pine nuts chopped, ½ cup almonds chopped, ½ cup pecans chopped, ¼ cup flax seeds, 2 tablespoons chia seeds, 1 large bell pepper any color chopped (red, orange, yellow, or green), 1 medium red or yellow onion chopped, 2 tablespoons sesame oil, ¼- ½ cup tahini, ¼ cup Bragg's Liquid Aminos or tamari sauce, 1 teaspoon red wine vinegar, 1 teaspoon salt, ½ teaspoon onion powder. (This is certainly enough for 2 people, but I still doubled everything so I would have some left over for lunch another day.)

Options: parsley would be great in this, or basil would be yummy.

Grilled asparagus: If you did not prepare extra butternut squash 3 nights ago.
Personal favorite: I like to dry-roast grains before putting them in the boiling liquid. This cooks off some of the sugars. In a large skillet on high heat, pour the grains in, stir occasionally being careful not to burn them. Once all the grains are a light brown color, remove from the heat. They are ready to be poured into the boiling liquid for the next cooking step.

Preparation, barley: Cook the barley by bringing 1 cup of water to boil, stir in the barley, cover, reduce to simmer, and cook for 20-23 minutes, or until the water is absorbed. If you are doubling the recipe, cook 1 cup of barley and use 2 cups of water. Set aside. If you cooked extra barley 2 nights ago, take it out of the refrigerator now.

Time-Saving Tip: If you didn't make extra barley 2 nights ago, make a little extra now for usage in 2 more days.

Preheat the oven to 350 degrees.

Place the chopped pine nuts, almonds, and pecans in a bowl. Put 1-2 tablespoons at a time into a coffee grinder or food processor, and make it into a fine ground. Place in another bowl and set aside. Grind the flax seeds and chia seeds and add to the ground nut mixture. Set aside.

Chop the bell pepper and onion and place in a separate large bowl. By hand, mix in the sesame oil, tahini, either Bragg's Liquid Aminos or tamari sauce, and the red wine vinegar and stir until well blended. Add the barley and stir again until well blended.

Begin adding the nut-seed mixture, stirring by hand, adding a little at a time, and continue stirring until well blended. Add the salt and onion powder, and parsley or basil at this point.

Line a baking sheet with foil. Make patties about the size of a regular burger and place on the sheet. Cook for 20 minutes, flip, and cook for 20 more. The burgers are done on each side when they are just slightly browned. Flip the patties delicately, as they break easily.

To complete your dinner, enjoy the cubed sautéed butternut squash from three nights ago or grilled asparagus.

Preparation, grilled asparagus: Wash a bundle of asparagus, chop off the back end, and place on a cookie sheet covered with foil. Drizzle with extra-virgin olive oil and grill on high. Check after 5-7 minutes and rotate, repeating so that all four sides are slightly charred.

"I feel good!"

_____
_____
_____
_____
_____
_____
_____
_____
_____

Day 14

Breakfast: 12 ounces water

7-Grain Cereal and Fruit

Ingredients: 4 ounces 7-grain hot cereal, 8 ounces water, ½ cup rice/coconut/almond/soy/hemp milk.

Preparation: Bring the water to a boil, then, while stirring, add the 7-grain cereal, bring to a boil again, then reduce to simmer, stirring often. When all the water is absorbed, remove from the heat, and pour into a bowl. After the grains are cooked you can add ½ cup of
the milk of your choice. For flavor options: add a sprinkle of cinnamon or all-spice.

If cantaloupe is in season, 2 slices of cantaloupe are a great compliment to this breakfast, otherwise, 1 apple or 1 pear.

The day is yours to grasp now that you have provided your body with all it needs to begin!

1 cup tea optional

Lunch: Quinoa Delight

Ingredients: 1 cup water, 1 teaspoon extra-virgin olive oil, ½ cup quinoa, ½ mango diced, 2 ounces almonds chopped, 1-2 ounces shredded coconut, 1 ounces dried cranberries, ¼ red onion diced, ½ red bell pepper diced, 1-2 ounces shredded carrots, 1 tablespoon ground flax seeds, cilantro dressing (recipe listed at the end of the Cleanse).

Time-Saving Tip: You can make an extra ½ cup of quinoa today and store it in the refrigerator for use for lunch on Day 20.

Personal favorite: I like to dry-roast grains before putting them in the boiling liquid. This cooks off some of the sugars. In a large skillet on high heat, pour the grains in, stir occasionally being careful not to burn them. Once all the grains are a light brown color, remove from the heat. They are ready to be poured into the boiling liquid for the next cooking step.

Preparation, quinoa: Pour 1 cup of water in a pot, then add the olive oil, and bring to boil. Stir in the quinoa, cover, reduce to simmer, and cook for 15-23 minutes, or until the water is absorbed.

Putting it all together: Put 1 cup of cooked quinoa in a bowl, layer in the mango, almonds, coconut, cranberries, red onion, bell pepper, carrots, and flax seeds, and drizzle on cilantro dressing and toss. Enjoy every colorful bite.

Dinner: Pasta With Pesto and Bruschetta

Ingredients, bruschetta: 16 ounces of sugar plum tomatoes diced, ½ cup parsley chopped, 3 cloves garlic minced, 1 cup fresh basil chopped, 3 tablespoons extra-virgin olive oil, pinch of   salt.

Options: ½ cup black olives diced; ½-1 red onion diced; 1 tablespoon balsamic vinegar; 1 cup mint diced instead of basil; 2 tablespoons fresh rosemary diced.

Time-Saving Tip: Dinner on Day 15 will be using this exact same bruschetta recipe. If you want, double the recipe for tonight and store half in the refrigerator to use tomorrow night.

Ingredients, pasta: 1 bag of gluten-free pasta, either quinoa, corn, rice, or spinach

Ingredients, pesto: 4 cloves garlic minced, 2 cups fresh basil chopped, 1 cup pine nuts, 1/3-½ cup extra-virgin olive oil, ½ teaspoon salt.

Time-Saving Tip: You will be using pesto with lunch on Day 17. You can increase the ingredients by 50%, allowing you enough for Day 17. If you choose to buy pre-made pesto, read the label, as most of the store-bought pesto sauces contain milk.

1 More needed ingredient: 1 box of Rice crackers.

Preparation, bruschetta: Place the diced sugar plum tomatoes, parsley, garlic, and basil in a bowl and mix together. If you are adding any of the options, put them in now and blend all the ingredients together. If you have time, let these ingredients sit together for 1 hour before cooking. If your schedule does not allow that, then just proceed to the cooking and your bruschetta will still taste great. Pour the olive oil in a pan and heat on high for 1-2 minutes. Pour the blended ingredients into the pan, sprinkle in the salt, and reduce heat to medium-high, and stir. Stir for 2 minutes, cooking only long enough for the tomatoes to just begin to break down. After 2 minutes remove the Bruschetta from the pan and let cool. Serve this at room temperature.

Preparation, pasta: Prepare the pasta as directed on the package.

Preparation, pesto: Place the garlic, basil, and pine nuts in a food processor or blender. Turn on and slowly drizzle in the olive oil. Blend until smooth. By adding the olive oil slowly, you get the perfect consistency. Pesto should be thick, not runny, yet pourable. Pour this into a bowl and stir in the salt. You can use this right away or store in the refrigerator for up to 3 days.

Putting it all together: Place the pasta in a large mixing bowl and pour the pesto over it and give it a toss. To enjoy the beautiful Bruschetta, spread the mix on top of the rice crackers.

Time-Saving Tip: If you want, you can even steam 3 cups of green beans tonight for tomorrow's dinner.
Night-Before Prep: Day 15 dinner is Cannellini Beans (white kidney beans). If using dried beans, soak them overnight. The recipe calls for 4 cups of cannellini beans.

Prep for tomorrow: Tomorrow's Potato Scramble breakfast takes a little more prep time than usual. If you have time tonight, cook the potatoes and refrigerate them, making sure you remove them from the boiling water before they get too soft or mushy. In the morning, start at the step where you place them in the skillet. Please refer to tomorrow's breakfast for cooking instructions.

"I feel good!"

_____

_____

_____

_____

_____

_____

_____

_____

Day 15

If you didn't soak your beans overnight, soak them this morning. Cannellini beans can be soaked for as little as 4 hours. The recipe calls for 4 cups of cannellini beans.

Breakfast: 12 ounces water

Ingredients: 6 medium red potatoes, 2 cups water, 1 tablespoon olive oil, ½ teaspoon salt, a sprinkle of pepper. Options: 1 ounce soy taco meat or soy chorizo, and 1 ounce fresh parsley chopped, or 1 teaspoon dried parsley flakes. If you are not using either soy product, you can use the parsley on its own or 1 ounce fresh basil chopped, or 1 teaspoon dried basil flakes. The soy product tastes great with parsley, not so much with basil. If you like red chili flakes, this is the perfect dish for that. Or even a hot sauce.

Preparation: Bring 2 cups of water to a boil. Wash the potatoes and cut in quarters, steam on high heat with a lid on for about 20 minutes, or until the potatoes are slightly soft but not fully cooked or mushy. Check every few minutes by sticking a fork in them. As the potatoes are just about finished cooking, turn on a skillet to high and pour the olive oil. Once the potatoes are slightly soft, remove them from the water and place them in the hot skillet. This would be the time to put the soy product in the skillet also. Stir the potatoes on high heat until they are browned; add in the parsley, or basil, and salt and pepper.

"Failure is success if we learn from it." – Malcolm Forbes

1 cup tea optional

Lunch: Barley With Hummus and Chopped Tomatoes

Ingredients: ½ cup pearl barley (you can replace the barley with quinoa or millet), 1 cup water, ½ teaspoon olive oil, ½ cup tomatoes chopped (any type, such as cherry, sugar plum, roma, or regular – my preference is sugar plum), 1-2 ounces of hummus

Personal favorite: I like to dry-roast grains before putting them in the boiling liquid. This cooks off some of the sugars. In a large skillet on high heat, pour the grains in, stir occasionally being careful not to burn them. Once all the grains are a light brown color, remove from the heat. They are ready to be poured into the boiling liquid for the next cooking step.

Ingredients Hummus: 15 ounces of cooked chick peas, 1 tablespoon extra virgin olive oil, 1 tablespoon water, 1/3 cup fresh lemon juice, 1 teaspoon salt. You can easily cook the chick peas by boiling them at a hard boil for 3 hours, or buy 1-15 ounce can. If the chick peas are canned, drain and rinse them off.

Hummus Time-Saving Tip: Many stores carry hummus in the refrigerator section. If time is a variable that gets short in your life, make this easy and go buy hummus at the store. My personal favorite is Garlic Hummus – Yum! You can eat hummus often throughout this cleanse as it is made from beans and is a very good source of healthy fats. You can snack on hummus as well as use it in meals.

Preparation, barley: In a pot with 1 cup of water, drizzle in the olive oil and bring to a boil, then stir in the barley, cover, reduce to simmer, and cook for 20-23 minutes, or until the water is absorbed. Set aside.

Preparation, hummus: Place all ingredients in a Vitamix® or blender and puree.

There are numerous variations on hummus:

For **garlic hummus**, add 2-3 large cloves of roasted garlic in before blending.

 For **roasted red bell pepper hummus**, add ½-1 whole roasted red bell pepper before blending.

For **olive hummus**, add ½ cup pitted olives before blending. With these variations, start with the lower amount of this extra ingredient and taste it before you increase the ingredient. For example, some people prefer a very garlicky flavor while others prefer just a subtle taste of garlic.

Putting it all together: In a bowl, place 1 cup of cooked barley or the grain you have chosen, add the cut tomatoes, and then 11-2 ounces of hummus. Toss this together like a salad. Enjoy this refreshing lunch!

Dinner: Red, White, and Green

Ingredients: 4 cups cannellini beans (white kidney beans), 4 cups steamed green beans, 2 cups bruschetta, ¾ cup diced marinated artichoke hearts, and ½-1 cup diced red onion (optional), 3/4 cup balsamic vinegar

Ingredients, bruschetta: Hopefully you made extra last night, if not here is what you will need: 16 ounces of sugar plum tomatoes diced, ½ cup parsley chopped, 3 cloves garlic minced, 1 cup fresh basil chopped, olive oil 3 tablespoon extra-virgin olive oil, pinch of salt

Options: ½ cup black olives diced; ½-1 red onion diced; 1 tablespoon balsamic vinegar; 1 cup mint diced instead of basil; 2 tablespoons fresh rosemary diced

Preparation, bruchetta: Place the diced sugar plum tomatoes, parsley, garlic, and basil in a bowl and mix together. If you are adding any of the options, put them in now and blend all the ingredients together. If you have time, let these ingredients sit together for 1 hour before cooking. If your schedule does not allow that, then just proceed to the cooking and your bruschetta will still taste great. Pour the olive oil in a pan and heat on high. Pour the blended ingredients into the pan, sprinkle in the salt, and reduce heat to medium-high, and stir. Stir for 2 minutes, cooking only long enough for the tomatoes to just begin to break down. After 2 minutes remove the Bruschetta from the pan and let cool. Serve this at room temperature.

Preparation, cannellini beans: If the Cannellini beans are soaking, drain and rinse the beans. If you did not soak the Cannellini beans, place them in a big pot, cover with water, bring to a boil, then reduce the heat, cover and simmer for about 1 hour, or until the beans are tender. Drain and rinse when cooked and place in the refrigerator or keep at room temperature.

Preparation, steamed green beans: In a second pot, bring 12 ounces of water to a boil. Break off the stem end of the green beans, wash the beans, and then place in boiling water. Cover and let steam for 6 minutes on high, stir once, then cover and steam another 4 minutes. Drain and cool under cold running water. Once cooled, cut the green beans into bit-size pieces, about 1 inch. Then place in refrigerator or serve these at room temperature, proceeding to the last step.

Putting it all together: In a large mixing bowl, layer in the cannellini beans, green beans, and bruschetta, add the diced artichoke hearts, and red onion (if you are using any), dress with balsamic vinegar, toss, and serve. This meal is good at room temperature, but is also nice if it is chilled. If you do have leftovers, refrigerate and try it chilled later.

"I feel good!"

_____

_____

_____

_____

_____

_____

_____

_____

_____

Day 16

Breakfast: 12 ounces water

Oatmeal and Fruit

Ingredients: 4 ounces oatmeal, 1 cup water, 1-2 ounces plain or vanilla soy/rice/coconut/almond/hemp milk, ½ banana sliced, and a sprinkle of cinnamon, or 1 ounce of a dried fruit (raisins, apricots, cranberries, blueberries)

Preparation: Bring the water to a boil, stir in the oatmeal. Keep at medium-high heat, stirring occasionally, until the oatmeal is the consistency you desire. Once the oatmeal is cooked, you can pour 1-2 ounce of plain or vanilla milk of your choice. Flavor options: ½ banana and a sprinkle of cinnamon; or 1 ounce of a dried fruit.

Enjoy. It's going to be a great day!

1 cup tea optional

Lunch: Rainbow of Yum!

I call this a "rainbow of yum" because it is a beautiful, very colorful salad. Because of all these different colors, it is loaded with a huge variety of phytonutrients for your body. My whole family loves this salad.

Ingredients: 2 cups arugula, 4 ounces pineapple diced, 4 ounces red cabbage diced or shredded, 2 ounces fennel diced, 2-4 ounces jicama diced, 2-4 ounces cucumber diced, 1 ounce green onion diced, sesame dressing (recipe listed earlier and at the end of the Cleanse)

Preparation: In a bowl place the arugula, pineapple, cabbage, fennel, jicama, cucumber, and green onions, dress with sesame dressing, toss, and enjoy!

Dinner: Roasted Red Bell Pepper and Fennel Risotto

Ingredients: 2 large red bell peppers, 2 bulbs fennel cut in half, 4 tablespoons extra-virgin olive oil, 3 cloves garlic diced, ¾ cup mushrooms diced (Portobello would add the most richness), 2 cups chopped tomatoes, 2 bay leaves, 4 cups vegetable stock, 1½ cups brown or Arborio rice, 6 fresh basil leaves chopped, 1/3 cup pine nuts, 1-2 teaspoons salt, 1-2 teaspoon pepper

Preparation: Preheat the broiler to high. Place the red bell peppers and fennel on a cookie sheet and drizzle with 2 tablespoons olive oil. Broil until blackened, but not completely burned, approximately 7 minutes, then rotate to another side, and repeat, until all sides are blackened. Immediately place the red bell pepper in a brown paper bag and let cool. Set the fennel aside to cool. Peel the skin from the bell peppers, remove the seeds, and dice. Cut the fennel into bite-size pieces.

In a wide cooking pot on high heat add the 2 tablespoons olive oil, garlic, mushrooms, and tomatoes, and cook over low heat for 5 minutes, stirring occasionally. At the same time, in a separate pot, heat the vegetable stock until it comes to a boil. Once boiling, reduce to simmer. Back at the first pot, stir the bell peppers and bay leaves into the garlic-mushroom-tomato mixture and cook on low for 15 minutes, stirring occasionally. After 15 minutes, stir in the rice and cook for 2 minutes, then uncover and increase the heat to medium. After 2 minutes, reduce the heat to low, and start slowly adding in the simmering stock 1 cup at a time. Stir occasionally, and cook until the stock is absorbed. Repeat until you have added all the stock and it has gotten absorbed. Remove from heat and stir in the pine nuts and roasted fennel, then salt and pepper to taste.

An option is to add red chili pepper flakes once the meal is cooked.

Night-Before Prep: Day 17 dinner is Black Beans, so if using dried beans soak them overnight.

Time-Saving Tip: Breakfast and dinner both require some cut-up vegetables, so if you need to, cut all the veggies up tonight making your morning easier.

"I feel good!"

_____

_____

_____

_____

_____

_____

_____

_____

_____

Day 17

Breakfast: 12 ounces water

Veggies and Grains

Ingredients: 4 ounces brown or white rice, 1 cup water, 1 teaspoon olive oil, 1 avocado diced, 2 ounces diced jicama, ½ bell pepper any color (green, yellow, red, or orange) diced, drizzle of balsamic vinaigrette

Preparation: In a pot with 1 cup of water, drizzle in the olive oil and bring to a boil, stir in the rice, cover, reduce to simmer, and cook for 20-23 minutes, or until the water is absorbed. While the rice is cooking, dice the avocado, jicama, and bell pepper. Once the rice is ready, place it in a bowl, putting the diced veggies on top, drizzle on the balsamic vinaigrette dressing, and enjoy a fabulous and very fresh breakfast!
You can either mix the vegetables into the rice or eat them separately.

Take a moment this morning to thank yourself for all you are doing to better yourself!

1 cup tea optional

Lunch: Multi-Grain Pesto, Avocado Sandwich

Ingredients: 2 pieces of wheat-free bread (kamut, spelt, rye, or multigrain), 1 avocado sliced, 1-2 ounces alfalfa sprouts, 1 ounces spinach or arugula, 2 radishes sliced, ¼ cup pesto

Ingredients, pesto: 4 cloves garlic minced, 2 cups fresh basil chopped, 1 cup pine nuts, 1/3- ½ cup extra-virgin olive oil, ½ teaspoon salt. If you choose to buy pre-made pesto, read the label. Most of the store-bought pesto sauces contain milk.

Preparation, pesto: Place the garlic, basil, and pine nuts in a food processor or blender. Turn on and slowly drizzle in the olive oil. Blend until smooth. By adding the olive oil slowly, you get the perfect consistency. Pesto should be thick, not runny, yet pourable. Pour this into a bowl and stir in the salt. You can use this right away or store in the refrigerator for up to 3 days.

Putting it all together Toast the 2 slices of bread, spread the pesto on each piece, layer on the alfalfa sprouts, radishes, spinach or arugula. Lay the slices of avocado on and top off with the other slice of toast.

Dinner: Black Beans

Ingredients: 2 tablespoons extra-virgin olive oil, ½ diced onion, 3 diced carrots, 3 stalks celery diced , 1 cup dried black beans, water or an organic vegetable stock, 1 teaspoon salt, ¼ teaspoon pepper, 1 bay leaf

Preparation: If you soaked the beans overnight, drain and rinse them and they are ready to be cooked.

If you did not soak the beans overnight, there is only a little difference in the cooking. Put 3 cups of water in a pot with the beans, cover, and bring to a boil. Keep at a hard boil for 10 minutes covered. Then, reduce the heat so the beans are simmering. Simmer covered for about 30 minutes or until the beans are tender. Drain the liquid off.

Preparation, crock pot: In a crock pot on high heat drizzle olive oil around the bottom and add the onion, carrots, and celery. Cook for 1 hour, then add 1 cup of dried black beans, cover with a liquid, either water or an organic vegetable stock. Sprinkle in salt, pepper, 1 bay leaf, and cook on high for 4 hours or low for 6 hours. This serves four.

Crock pot variation: If your need to get out of the house in the morning, add all the ingredients into the crock pot at the same time. Cook on high for 4-5 hours or low for 6 hours. Your beans will still taste absolutely perfect!

Preparation, stovetop: In a stovetop pot, sauté the onion, carrots, and celery in olive oil until softened, then add the other ingredients, bring to a boil, then reduce the heat and simmer for 2 hours.

You will be having these black beans for lunch on Day 19.

"I feel good!"

_____

_____

_____

_____

_____

_____

_____

_____

_____

Day 18

Breakfast: 12 ounces water

Quesadilla
"I get a quesadilla on a vegan cleanse!?" Yes, you do!

Ingredients: 2 corn tortillas, 2 ounces shredded soy, rice, or vegan cheese (American, mozzarella, or cheddar flavored), 1 avocado sliced. **Options:** 1 bell pepper any color chopped; 1 ounce red onion diced; 1 medium tomato chopped, or salsa; 1 ounce jicama chopped

Preparation: Put the 2 corn tortillas on a broiler pan. Spread the options you've chosen onto each tortilla then layer on the shredded cheese. Under the broiler, on high, cook the quesadillas until the cheese has melted, about 2-4 minutes. Top with the sliced avocado.

Yummy for your tummy! And your brain, and you immune system, and your liver, and on and on…

1 cup tea optional

Lunch: Colorful Cabbage Salad
Another of my favorites. (I have a lot of favorites!)

Ingredients: 5 cups shredded green cabbage, 1 cup shredded red cabbage, 1-2 medium-size tomatoes diced, 1 avocado diced, ½ cup diced onion any color, 1-2 limes juiced, ½ teaspoon salt, ¼ teaspoon ground pepper (optional)

Preparation: In a large mixing bowl blend all ingredients together. Toss the salad after adding the lime juice and salt and pepper. Refrigerate for minimum 30 minutes. Serve chilled.   This is very easy to prepare ahead of time and take to work. This is also a very refreshing salad on a hot summer night.

Dinner: Grilled Cheese With Apple Slices and Grilled Fennel

This is a great meal for a Saturday or Sunday evening. If this day in your Cleanse does not fall on a Saturday or Sunday, feel free to switch the recipe from one of those days with this.

Ingredients: 2 pieces of wheat-free bread (kamut, spelt, rye or multigrain), 2 pieces of a dairy-free cheese, ½ apple any color cut into thin slices, 1 fennel bulb, 1 tablespoon extra-virgin olive oil, drizzle of balsamic vinegar. Option to use a little canola oil margarine.

It is best to prepare the grilled fennel first, prepping the ingredients for the grilled cheese sandwich while the fennel is grilling.

Preparation, grilled fennel: Wash and split the fennel bulb in half. Place the halves on a cookie sheet and drizzle with extra-virgin olive oil. With the broiler on high and the rack in the middle of the oven, broil for about 15 minutes, checking periodically. The fennel should be browned but not burned. Turn the fennel over and broil the other side for 12-15 minutes. Once completely grilled, set aside and let cool. Dice the grilled fennel, place it in a bowl and drizzle on a little balsamic vinegar and toss. Set aside until your grilled cheese sandwich is ready.

Preparation, grilled cheese sandwich: Toast the 2 pieces of bread only slightly (this makes for shorter grilling time). On a cookie sheet, place the slightly toasted bread, layer on a thin amount of canola oil margarine if so desired, place 1 piece of the dairy-free cheese on each piece of toast, and place under the boiler. The lower setting on the broiler is best for this and the rack should be set in the middle of the oven so the heat source is not too close; keep a watch on it so as not to burn it. Slice an apple into thin slices. Once the cheese has melted, layer the apple slices on top of 1 of the pieces with the melted cheese. Top off with the other toast slice to make a sandwich.

Preparation, grilled fennel: Place your grilled fennel into a bowl, and enjoy as the side dish with the grilled cheese and apple sandwich.

Over-night prep: if you do not have black beans left over from Day 17 dinner, plan ahead for tomorrow's lunch by soaking the black beans overnight. Notice that cooking time for these beans could take as long as 4 hours, which is why this meal was placed as lunch on Day 19, with the hopes that you had some of the black beans left over from Day 17

"I feel good!"

_____
_____
_____
_____
_____
_____
_____
_____
_____

Day 19

Breakfast: 12 ounces water

Toast, Hummus, Smoothie (THS)

Ingredients: 2 pieces of a wheat-free bread (kamut, spelt, multigrain, or rye), 2 ounces hummus, 1 protein smoothie of your choice (all smoothies recipes are at the end)

Ingredients Hummus: 15 ounces of cooked chick peas, 1 tablespoon extra virgin olive oil, 1 tablespoon water, 1/3 cup fresh lemon juice, 1 teaspoon salt. You can easily cook the chick peas by boiling them at a hard boil for 3 hours, or buy 1-15 ounce can. If the chick peas are canned, drain and rinse them off.

Hummus Time-Saving Tip: Many stores carry hummus in the refrigerator section. If time is a variable that gets short in your life, make this easy and go buy hummus at the store. My personal favorite is Garlic Hummus – Yum! You can eat hummus often throughout this cleanse as it is made from beans and is a very good source of healthy fats. You can snack on hummus as well as use it in meals.

Preparation, hummus: Place all ingredients in a Vitamix® or blender and puree.
There are numerous variations on hummus:
For **garlic hummus**, add 2-3 large cloves of roasted garlic in before blending.
 For **roasted red bell pepper hummus**, add ½-1 whole roasted red bell pepper before blending.

For **olive hummus**, add ½ cup pitted olives before blending. With these variations, start with the lower amount of this extra ingredient and taste it before you increase the ingredient. For example, some people prefer a very garlicky flavor while others prefer just a subtle taste of garlic.

Putting it all together: Toast 2 pieces of a wheat-free bread and spread hummus on top. Make 1 protein smoothie of your choice.

A powerful breakfast for a powerful day!

1 cup tea optional

Lunch: Quinoa, Black Beans, Corn, and Pico de Gallo

Ingredients: ½ cup uncooked quinoa, 1 cup water, ½ teaspoon olive oil, 4 ounces black beans, 4 ounces corn cooked, 3 ounces Pico de Gallo

Ingredients, Pico de Gallo: ½ pound plum tomatoes, ¼ cup chopped red onion, 1 ounce chopped cilantro , 1 tablespoon lime or lemon juice (lime juice will make it tangier, lemon juice is not as tangy but still has bite to it)

Optional: 1 tablespoon minced and seeded jalapeño peppers, 1 teaspoon-1 tablespoon minced garlic, to your taste, or it keep out entirely

If you did not make extra quinoa 5 days ago, then prepare your quinoa now.

Personal favorite: I like to dry-roast grains before putting them in the boiling liquid. This cooks off some of the sugars. In a large skillet on high heat, pour the grains in, stir occasionally being careful not to burn them. Once all the grains are a light brown color, remove from the heat. They are ready to be poured into the boiling liquid for the next cooking step.

Preparation, quinoa: Cook the quinoa by bringing 1 cup of water to boil, stir in the quinoa, cover, reduce to simmer, and cook for 15-23 minutes, or until the water is absorbed.

Hopefully you have black beans from Day 17 dinner. If not, here is the recipe:

Preparation, black beans: If you soaked the beans overnight, drain them and cook them (you will need 4 ounces). If you did not do the overnight soak, do a quick soak by boiling them in water for 1 hour, drain, and then cook. To cook the black beans, in a pot with 8-12 ounces of water, drizzle in olive oil and bring to a boil, add the beans to the boiling water, and cook on high covered for approximately 4 hours.

Black beans Time-Saving Tip: You can buy a can of organic black beans and use 4 ounce for this meal.

Preparation, corn: Get 1 ear of corn, though you will only be using 4 ounces for this lunch, you can use any corn left-over in tomorrow's lunch. You can roast the corn or boil it.

To roast: Place the corn on a cookie sheet and drizzle with extra-virgin olive oil. With the broiler on high and the rack in the middle of the oven, broil for about 12 minutes, checking periodically. The corn should be browned but not burned. Rotate the corn and broil another side for 12 minutes. Continue until all sides are charred.

If boiling the corn, bring 3 cups of water to a boil, place the corn in the boiling water and cover. Let this boil for just 7-10 minutes. Remove from the boiling water and let cool. Once the corn has cooled from either cooking method, cut the corn off the cob.

Preparation, Pico de Gallo: In a bowl, combine all ingredients and toss together.

Pico de Gallo Time-Saving Tip: You can buy a Pico de Gallo at most grocery stores, saving yourself a lot of time.
Make this meal fast and easy by using either leftover or canned beans, plus store-bought Pico de Gallo. Once you see how fast and easy this meal can be, you might decide to keep it in your lifestyle!

Putting it all together: Place the quinoa in a bowl, layer on the black beans, 4 ounces of corn and then top off with the Pico de Gallo. This is a meal that should keep you satisfied for hours. It fuels your brain with its rich supply of highly usable phytonutrients.

Dinner: Stir Fry Vegetables

Ingredients: 2 tablespoons sesame oil; 3 bundles of miniature bok choy; 6 ounces sliced mushrooms; 3 carrots sliced; 7 radishes sliced; 1 red onion diced; 2 zucchini sliced; 1 bell pepper, any color, sliced; 1/2 cup broccoli sliced to bite-size pieces; 1/2 cup cauliflower sliced to bite-size pieces; 1/2 cup green beans sliced to bite-size pieces; 1/2 cup sugar snap peas cut into bite-size pieces; 3 cloves of garlic diced. This list of vegetables was purposely made to include a wide variety. Since it is a large list of vegetables, and will yield a lot of stir fry, it can be changed according to your own taste. Feel free to delete whichever ones you do not like. As listed, this will make enough to easily feed a family of four and still have some left over.

Brown rice or white rice: 2 cup water, 1 cup brown or white rice, ½ teaspoon sesame oil

Preparation, rice: Start cooking the rice first, so that by the time you have cooked the veggies, the rice will be done. Pour 2 cups of water in a pot, add the sesame oil, and bring to a boil. Pour in the rice and cook according to the directions on the package, usually 20-30 minutes.

Preparation, stir fry: In a wok or large skillet, turn heat on high and pour in the sesame oil, allowing 2 minutes to heat up. Put all the cut-up vegetables into the wok or skillet and cover. Reduce heat to medium-high, stirring every 2 minutes, and replacing the lid. Continue this until the vegetables have either the crispness or softness you desire. Crispy vegetables will take approximately 12-15 minutes, softer veggies will need to cook longer.

Putting it all together: In a bowl, put a ¼ cup of cooked rice, layer on the vegetables, and add tamari sauce or Bragg's Liquid Aminos, if desired.

"I feel good!"

_____

_____

_____

_____

_____

_____

_____

_____

Day 20

Breakfast: 12 ounces water

Barley +

Ingredients: 3 ounces uncooked pearl barley (3 ounces uncooked barley will yield 6 ounces of cooked barley), 6 ounces of water, ½ teaspoon olive oil, 1 teaspoon canola margarine. Optional additions for this morning are 1 handful of dried cranberries, and 1 handful of pine nuts; or 1 handful of dried pomegranate seeds and 1 handful of diced cashews. This is really great! You could even sprinkle cinnamon or all-spice on this. One more option, and a great way to get your essential fatty acids, is to sprinkle on 2 tablespoons of ground flax seeds, which will give this a nutty flavor.

Personal favorite: I like to dry-roast grains before putting them in the boiling liquid. This cooks off some of the sugars. Pour the grains into a large skillet on high heat, stirring occasionally and making sure not to burn the grains. Once all the grains are a light brown color, remove from the heat, and hold aside until the next cooking step.

Preparation, barley: Pour the water in a pot, pour in ½ teaspoon olive oil, and bring to a boil. Stir in the barley, cover and simmer for 20-23 minutes, or until the water is absorbed.
In a bowl place 6 ounces of hot barley. While the barely is hot, mix in a little canola margarine to moisten. Top off with any of the options you want and enjoy!

Insanity is doing the same thing over and over again and expecting different results."– Albert Einstein.

The Standard American Diet has proven to be harmful to the human body, causing chronic health problems and leaving millions of Americans on pharmaceutical medications for life. This Cleanse will help you can break this cycle!

1 cup tea optional

Lunch: Vegan Tacos

Ingredients: 2 corn tortillas, 2 ounces lettuce or mixed field greens, 1 avocado sliced, ½ cucumber sliced, 1-2 ounces jicama slices, 1 ounce fresh tomatoes sliced or salsa or Pico de Gallo, 1 ounce corn, 1 ounce mango pieces or pineapple pieces diced. Option to top this off with the cilantro dressing.

Pick any of these ingredients you want from the list above, they all taste beautiful together in any combination!

Putting it all together: Place the 2 corn tortillas on a plate, layer on the lettuce or mixed field greens and then continue layering on all of the other ingredients. Drizzle the cilantro dressing on top if you'd like. (Cilantro dressing listed earlier and at the end of the Cleanse.)
This is easy to take to work. Just place each of the ingredients you want separate little containers. At lunchtime, simply put the vegan tacos together and, voila, you have a yummy healthy lunch!

Dinner: Rich Couscous and Portobello Mushrooms

Ingredients: 1 cup uncooked couscous (couscous is wheat, but it is a whole grain, not a processed wheat product), 5 cups water, 2 tablespoons extra-virgin olive oil, ½ cup red onion diced, 1 tablespoon garlic diced, 2 Portobello mushrooms diced, 1-2 ounces pine nuts

Preparation, couscous: In a tea kettle, bring the water to a boil. In a large skillet on high heat, drizzle in the olive oil and heat for 1 minute, add in the onion and garlic, and sauté on medium heat for about 5 minutes, stirring almost continuously. Add the diced Portobello mushrooms and sauté for another 2 minutes, stirring continuously. Add the couscous and continue to sauté for 2 more minutes, stirring continuously. After 2 minutes, pour in 2 ½ cups of boiling water, bring the entire mixture to a boil, cover; reduce the heat so the couscous is just at a simmer. Simmer for 10-15 minutes. Sprinkle with pine nuts once the couscous has been placed in a bowl. This is a very rich and satisfying meal. Enjoy!

"I feel good!"

_____

_____

_____

_____

_____

_____

_____

_____

Day 21

Breakfast: 12 ounces water

7-Grain Cereal and Fruit

Ingredients: 4 ounces 7-grain hot cereal, 1 cup water, ½ cup soy/rice/coconut/almond/hemp milk. Pick 1 fruit option: ½ banana sliced; or 1 ounce of fresh raspberries, or blueberries, or 1 ounce of dried fruit, such as raisins, apricots (chop the dried apricots into bite-size pieces), a sprinkle of cinnamon.

Preparation: Bring the water to a boil and stir in the 7- grain cereal, keeping heat at medium-high. Stir occasionally until the water is absorbed. Once the cereal is cooked, pour it into a bowl, add your milk and fruit of choice, and a sprinkle of cinnamon.

A breakfast to fuel your heart!

1 cup tea optional

Lunch: Kale Salad

Ingredients: 2 cups of kale cut into bite-size pieces, 1 cup shredded green cabbage, ½ cup carrots shredded, 1 handful dried cranberries, 1 handful dried pomegranate seeds, sesame or peanut dressing (recipes for both are listed at the end)

Preparation: Kale is a highly nutritious deep green that is also very fibrous. To be able to eat kale raw, the trick is in marinating it. After washing and cutting up the kale, pour the dressing on it and set it aside for a minimum 30 minutes, literally; the kale could marinate for even a few hours and would be great. After marinating, place the kale in a mixing bowl, add the other ingredients, toss together, and enjoy.

Dinner: Butternut Squash and Crimmini Mushroom Soup

Ingredients: 1 ½ tablespoon extra-virgin olive oil, 1 medium butternut squash peeled and cubed (or buy 2 packages of cubed butternut squash), 1 box of Crimmini mushrooms diced, 2 tablespoons minced garlic, 1 large red onion diced, 1 container (32 ounces) organic vegetable stock, ½-1 teaspoon salt and ¼-1/2 teaspoon pepper

Preparation: Drizzle 1 ½ tablespoons olive oil into crock pot, add the butternut squash, mushrooms, garlic, red onions, and organic vegetable stock, add salt and pepper. Cook on high for 6 hours. When cooked, blend all these ingredients together using a Vitamix®, a stand-up blender, or a hand-held blender, and blend until all the ingredients have become liquefied. This serves 4 people.

This is yummy! I hope you brought your appetite and some wonderful company to share this with!

Night-Before Prep: Day 22 dinner is Green Mung Beans. If using dried beans, soak them overnight.

Time-Saving Tip: if you need to, cut all the veggies up tonight making your morning easier.

"I feel good!"

_____

_____

_____

_____

_____

_____

_____

_____

_____

_____

Day 22

Breakfast: 12 ounces water

Fruit Salad

Ingredients: ½ banana sliced, 6 strawberries sliced, 1-2 ounces grapes sliced.
Options: replace the grapes with ½ mango sliced; replace the grapes with 1-2 ounces blueberries; replace the grapes with 1-2 ounces raspberries.

Preparation: Place your cut-up fruit choices in a bowl and mix.

Even more options: have just 2 of the fruits and 1 piece of toast (kamut, spelt, rye, or multigrain).

"Do you feel it? Do you feel how powerful you are when you can make the best choices for yourself?!"

1 cup tea optional

Lunch: Fennel, Mushroom, Tomato, and Barley

Ingredients: 1 fennel bulb diced, 4 button mushrooms diced, 1 medium tomato diced, 1 ½ tablespoons extra-virgin olive oil, ½ cup uncooked pearl barley, 1 cup water, pinch of salt, pinch of pepper

Preparation, barley: Pour the water in a pot, add 1/2 tablespoon of the olive oil, and bring to a boil. Stir in the barley. Reduce heat to low, cover, and keep at a simmer for about 20-23 minutes, or until the water is absorbed.

Preparation, vegetables: In a skillet on high heat, pour in 1 tablespoon olive oil and heat for about 1 minute. Place the cut fennel, mushrooms, and tomatoes in the pan, reduce heat to medium-high, and sauté for about 5 minutes, stirring often.

Putting it all together: In a bowl, place the cooked barley, and layer on the fennel, mushrooms, and tomatoes. Salt and pepper to taste.

Dinner: Mung Beans

Green mung beans are another one of my absolute favorite dishes! You can buy them from any store that sells Indian food.

Ingredients: 2 cups green mung beans, 2 tablespoons extra-virgin olive oil, 2-4 cloves garlic minced, 3 large stalks of celery chopped, 3 large carrots chopped, 1 medium red onion chopped, 16 ounces organic vegetable stock, 1-2 cups water, 2 teaspoons cumin, 2 teaspoons turmeric, 2 teaspoons cardamom (the latter three ingredients are also available at Indian grocers), 1-2 teaspoons salt

Crock pot preparation: In a crock pot turned to high, pour in the olive oil, and heat for 2 minutes. Next, add in the garlic, celery, carrots, and onion, stirring the mixture until all the ingredients are blended. Cover and let cook for 1 hour. After 1 hour, place the beans into the crock pot and pour the vegetable stock and then enough water to cover the beans. Add the cumin, turmeric, cardamom, salt, and pepper, and stir until everything is well blended. Cook on high for 4-5 hours or on low for 6 hours.

Crock pot variation: If you need to just put all the ingredients in the crock pot in the morning and head out the door that would still be fine. Your mung beans will still taste great.

Stovetop preparation: If you will be cooking this on the stovetop, on high heat, add extra-virgin olive oil and heat for 1-2 minutes. Add the garlic, celery, carrots, and onion, stirring the mixture for 7-10 minutes. Pour the beans into the stock pot, then pour in the vegetable stock and enough water to cover the beans. Add the cumin, turmeric, cardamom, salt, and pepper, and stir until everything is well blended. Cook on high until it reaches a boil, then reduce to low-medium heat to simmer for 4 hours, string occasionally.

"I feel good!"

Day 23

Breakfast: 12 ounces water

Yogurt and Fruit

Ingredients: Yogurt options: soy or almond, any flavor. Fruit options: pick any 2 fresh fruits form this list: ½ banana sliced, ½ pear sliced, ½ apple sliced, 10 grapes sliced, 8 strawberries sliced, 15 blueberries, 15 raspberries.

Pour the yogurt into a bowl, top with the 2 fruits of your choice, and enjoy!

A day of joy awaits you!

1 cup tea optional

Lunch: Beet Salad

My Mom used to make this and I always loved the great flavors!

Ingredients: 4 large beets sliced, 1 red onion diced, 2-3 tablespoons red wine vinegar, ½ teaspoon dried parsley flakes, olive oil, salt and pepper to taste

Preparation: In a large pot, pour 3 cups of water and bring to a boil. Put the cut beets in and steam covered for about 15 minutes or until tender but not mushy. Remove from the stove, drain, and run under cold water. Cut the beets into bite-size pieces. In a large mixing bowl, put the beets and red onions, drizzle on the vinegar, olive oil, and sprinkle on the parsley flakes, salt, and pepper. Toss together. This can be eaten at room temperature or cold. It is really good chilled!

Dinner: Polenta With a Rainbow

Ingredients, polenta: 4 cup water, 1 ½ cup organic polenta. This will make enough for 4-8 people.

Time-Saving Tip: Buy one 18-ounce tube organic polenta (buy 2 if you are feeding 4 people)

Ingredients, the rainbow: 2 tablespoons canola oil margarine or any dairy-free margarine you prefer, 1 cup mushrooms sliced, ½ cup red onions sliced, 12 ounces organic vegetable broth, 1 cup organic sugar plum tomatoes sliced, ½ cup artichoke hearts sliced, 1 ounce capers. To serve 4, double all of the above, **except** the vegetable stock. You may need a little more vegetable stock than 12 ounces, but most likely not 24 ounces.

Preparation, polenta: Pour the 4 cups of water in a big pot on high heat and bring the water to a boil, then reduce to simmer. While stirring, slowly add the polenta. A whisk for stirring helps prevent clumps. Continue stirring the polenta until it is thick and pulls away from the sides of the pan, 20-50 minutes. Pour the polenta onto a wooden cutting board; do not pour the polenta on to a plastic cutting board and shape into a square. Let the polenta cool and settle for a few minutes and then cut it into 1" thick slices in order to prepare it for the next cooking step.

Putting the rainbowl together: Put the canola oil margarine in a large skillet and heat on high for 1-2 minutes, just enough to heat it up but not burn it. Add in the mushrooms and red onions, reduce the heat to medium, and sauté for about 5 minutes, stirring at 1-minute intervals. Add the vegetable broth and increase to high heat for about 2 minutes. Reducing the heat back to medium, add the slices of polenta, and cook for about 10 minutes. Then flip the polenta, add the sliced tomatoes, and cook for 5 minutes. For the last 5 minutes, add on top the artichoke hearts and for the last 1 minute, add the capers.

Night-Before Prep: Day 24 dinner is Cannellini Beans (white kidney beans). If using dried beans, soak 2 cups of them overnight.

Time-Saving Tip: You can buy 1 can of white beans.

"I feel good!"

_____

_____

_____

_____

_____

_____

_____

_____

_____

Day 24

Day 25 breakfast requires a baked apple. Bake the apple today or tonight so it is ready for you in the morning for breakfast.

Preparation, baked apple: Preheat oven to 350 degrees, wrap the apple in foil, and bake for 40 minutes. Store in the refrigerator. A red or green apple is fine. Organic apples are best. You can bake a few apples and store them to eat over the next 3-5 days, as they make a delicious snack or dessert.

Tonight's dinner is Cannellini Beans. If you did not soak your beans overnight, soak 2 cups of dried beans this morning. Cannellini beans can be soaked for as little as 4 hours.

Breakfast: 12 ounces water

Power Toast

Ingredients: 2 pieces of wheat-free bread (kamut, spelt, rye or multigrain), 2 teaspoons peanut butter, and 1 banana sliced. Protein smoothie of your choice (smoothie recipes are listed at the end).

Preparation: Toast the 2 pieces of bread, spread with peanut butter, and top with banana slices, on each piece. Prepare protein smoothie of your choice per recipe at end.

As this food nourishes your body, your mind is nourished. This sets you up for a bright day!

1 cup tea optional

Lunch: Roasted Parsnips, Carrots, and Potatoes

This is a yummy and easy-to-prepare lunch.

Ingredients: 1 potato cut into bit- size pieces, 1 tablespoon extra-virgin olive oil, 2 parsnips peeled and cut into bite-size pieces, 2 carrots peeled and cut into bite-size pieces, ¼ cup fresh parsley diced, salt and pepper to taste.

Preparation: Pre-heat the oven to 325 degrees. In a large roasting pan place the potatoes and drizzle on ½ tablespoon olive oil. Mix this together so all the potatoes get coated. Cook for 30 minutes. Then add in the parsnips and carrots, drizzle on the other ½ tablespoon olive oil and mix together again coating all the vegetables. Return to the oven and cook for 20 minutes more, stirring 10 minutes after placing it in the oven. The parsnips and carrots will be crunchier. If you want them softer, place them in at the beginning and cook them with the potatoes the entire time. Once everything is cooked to your liking, sprinkle on the parsley, and salt and pepper. Toss this altogether and enjoy.

Dinner: Cannellini Beans (White Kidney Beans) With Spinach.

Ingredients: 2 cup dried Cannellini white beans, 1 tablespoon extra-virgin olive oil, 3-5 cloves garlic minced, 4-6 tablespoons chopped red onions, 2 teaspoons salt, 6 cups organic vegetable stock or water, 20 ounces diced tomatoes, 2 cups chopped spinach, salt and pepper to taste

If you soaked the beans overnight, drain and rinse them. If you did not soak the beans overnight, do a quick soak: Place the beans and enough water to cover them in a pot, bring to a boil, and keep at a hard boil covered for 10 minutes. Drain the beans from this water and proceed with the next step.

Time-Saving Tip: Buy 1 can of white beans.

Preparation: Pour the olive oil in a large cooking pan and heat on high 1-2 minutes Add the garlic, onions, and salt, stirring for 2 minutes on medium-high heat. Add the vegetable stock or water and bring to a boil. Add the beans and once it begins to boil, reduce heat to low, and simmer covered for 1 hour, or until the beans are soft enough for eating. Keeping the heat on low, add the diced tomatoes and spinach, and stir them in until the spinach is completely softened. This takes maybe 2 minutes. Flavor with salt and pepper.

"I feel good!"

_____

_____

_____

_____

_____

_____

_____

_____

_____

Day 25

Breakfast: 12 ounces water

7-Grain Hot Cereal With Baked Apple and Cinnamon

Ingredients: 4 ounces of 7-grain hot cereal, 1 cup water, 1 baked apple chopped, ½ to 1 ounce soy/rice/coconut/almond/hemp milk (your preference), sprinkle of cinnamon

Preparation, baked apple: Preheat oven to 350 degrees, wrap the apple in foil, and bake for 40 minutes. A red or green apple is fine. Organic apples are best.

Putting it all together: Bring water to a boil, while stirring, add the 7-grain cereal, bring to a boil then reduce to simmer, stirring often. When almost all the water is absorbed, add the chopped baked apple, stirring. Cook until all the water is absorbed or until desired thickness. Once the cereal is cooked, you can pour ½ to 1 ounce of soy/rice/coconut/almond/hemp milk over it and add a sprinkle of cinnamon. You have a super breakfast!

"The important thing in life is to have a great aim, and the determination to attain it." – Johann Wolfgang von Goethe

1 cup tea optional

Lunch: Rice Noodles and Veggies

Ingredients, veggies: 1 tablespoon sesame oil, ½ onion chopped, 2 leeks thinly sliced, 1 tablespoon fresh ginger grated, 1 tablespoon garlic diced, 2 tablespoons tamari sauce or Bragg's Liquid Aminos, 1 tablespoon rice wine vinegar, ½ cup carrots diced, ½ cup green cabbage diced, ½ cup edamame beans fresh or frozen

Ingredients, rice noodles: 8 ounces rice noodles, 4 cups water, salt and pepper to taste

Preparation, veggies: In a skillet on high, pour in the sesame oil and heat for 1-2 minutes. Add the onion, leeks, ginger, and garlic, and reduce the heat to medium. Cook for about 5 minutes, stirring occasionally. Add the tamari sauce or Bragg's Liquid Aminos, rice wine vinegar, carrots, cabbage, and edamame beans, cover and cook for 10 minutes, stirring occasionally.

Preparation, rice noodles: While the veggies are cooking, in a separate pot, bring the water to a boil. Once boiling, put the rice noodles in the water and cook for approximately 3 minutes. Rice noodles cook very quickly. If the package has different directions, follow them. Drain the noodles and place in a large bowl. Add the cooked veggies and salt and pepper, toss together.

Dinner: Potato Lentil Patties

Ingredients: 2 potatoes cubed, 4 quarts water, 1 tablespoon canola oil margarine, ¼ cup plain coconut milk (unflavored), ½ cup dried brown lentils, ½ cup red onion diced, 2 tablespoons garlic diced, ½ cup celery diced, 1 tablespoon olive oil (this is only if you will be sautéing the onion, garlic, and celery), ½ cup sunflower seeds, ½ cup pecans or walnuts ground

Preparation, potatoes: Bring 2 quarts of water to a boil. Place the cubed potatoes in the water and cook at a boil for about 20 minutes on high, covered, or until the potatoes are soft. Check them with a fork. Drain the potatoes and place them in a large mixing bowl. Add the canola oil margarine and coconut milk and either mash by hand or use a handheld blender to make mashed potatoes. Set aside.

Preparation, lentils: Bring 2 quarts of water to a boil, place the lentils in, and cover, cook at a boil for about 30 minutes. Drain and set aside.
Preheat the oven to 350 degrees.

Option: You have the option to sauté the onion, garlic, and celery at this time. If you would like to keep them raw then skip this step. (I personally like them raw in this dish.) If sautéing, in a skillet with heat on high, pour in the olive oil and heat for 1-2 minutes. Place the onion, garlic, and celery in and sauté on medium heat for about 5 minutes, stirring occasionally. Remove from heat and set aside.

Putting it all together: To the mashed potatoes, add the lentils, sunflower seeds, pecans or walnuts, and onion, garlic, celery, salt and pepper to taste. Mix together until blended evenly. Form into patties about the size of a regular burger. Line a baking sheet with foil, and place the patties on the sheet. Cook for 15 minutes, flip and cook for 15 more. They are done on each side when they are just slightly browned. Flip the patties delicately, they break easily.

"I feel good!"

_____

_____

_____

_____

_____

_____

_____

_____

_____

Day 26

Breakfast: 12 ounces water

Oatmeal and Fruit

Ingredients: 4 ounces of oatmeal, 1 cup water, ½- 1 ounce of soy/rice/coconut/almond/hemp milk. For flavor options: ½ banana sliced, or 5 strawberries sliced, or 8 raspberries, or 10 blueberries, or ¼ diced apple

Preparation: Bring the water to a boil, while stirring add the oatmeal and return to a boil, reduce to a simmer, stirring often. Cook until all the water is absorbed or until desired thickness. Once the cereal is cooked, add the milk and fruit of choice and enjoy!

Good food makes you feel good . . . And that's what it's all about!

1 cup tea optional

Lunch: Grilled Asparagus With Artichokes

Ingredients: 1 bundle of asparagus, 1 teaspoon olive oil, ½ cup marinated artichoke hearts diced, 1 tomato diced, balsamic vinegar or balsamic vinaigrette dressing

Grilling the asparagus: Place the asparagus on a broiling pan, drizzle on the olive oil, and roll to coat the stalks. Broil on high heat for about 7 minutes, rotate, and broil another 7 minutes, rotate again and broil for about 5 minutes (three times total). They are done when all sides are just slightly charred.

Preparation: Once the asparagus has cooled, cut 8 stalks of asparagus into bite-size pieces and put in a mixing bowl. Store the rest of the grilled asparagus in the refrigerator for lunch tomorrow. Add the marinated artichoke hearts and tomatoes, drizzle with either balsamic vinegar or balsamic vinaigrette dressing. Toss this all together and yum!

Dinner: Garlic Rice, Broccoli, and Tofu

Ingredients: 1 ½ cups water, 2 tablespoons extra-virgin olive oil, 2 tablespoons garlic minced, ½ cup uncooked rice, 4 ounces broccoli separated into florets, 14 ounces firm tofu drained and cubed

Time-Saving Tip: Tomorrow's lunch calls for either broccoli or cauliflower steamed. If you like broccoli, cook an extra 6 ounces of broccoli florets now and it will be ready for your lunch tomorrow. If making the extra broccoli, add more 1 cup of water when steaming the broccoli.

Preparation, garlic rice: Pour 2 cups of water in a tea kettle and bring up to a boil. While the water is being heated, in a skillet on high heat, drizzle 1 tablespoon olive oil in and heat for about 1-2 minutes, then add the garlic and sauté stirring for about 2 minutes, then add the rice and stir another 2 minutes. Pour in 1 cup of boiling water and cover, return to a boil, then reduce the heat to low and simmer for 12-23 minutes (this would depend on the type of rice you have – consult the rice package for cooking time). Set aside.

Preparation, broccoli: In a separate pot, bring 4 ounces of water to a boil. Add the broccoli and steam covered for about 4-6 minutes, or until desired crunchiness. It is definitely better to cook your vegetables for a short amount of time, leaving them crunchy and full of nutrients. Set aside. If you steamed tomorrow's broccoli too, place it off to the side. Once cooled store it in the refrigerator.

Preparation, sautéed tofu: Take a 14-ounce container of firm tofu, and cut it into cubes. In a skillet on high heat drizzle in 1 tablespoon olive oil, heat for about 1 minute, then add the cubed tofu, reduce heat to medium-high, and sauté for about 5 minutes, stirring at 1 minute intervals. Dinner for Day 29 has the option to use sautéed tofu, so go ahead and sauté the whole 14-ounce package of firm tofu tonight if you would like some in 3 nights.

Putting it all together: In a bowl combine 1 cup cooked rice, 4 ounces steamed broccoli, 4 ounces sautéed tofu, and toss together. You can drizzle tamari sauce or Bragg's Liquid Aminos on this or a little sesame dressing. If possible do not use soy sauce as this contains wheat.

Night-Before Prep: Tomorrow's dinner is 17 Bean Soup, so soak the beans overnight.

"I feel good!"

Day 27

Breakfast: 12 ounces water

Congee
When cooking grains, if you add more liquid and cook them longer than what the usual recipe calls for, you end up making what is called "congee" in Chinese medicine. Congee is very nurturing for your immune system and the spleen.

Ingredients: 3 ounces brown or white rice, 6 ounces water, 3 ounces of either plain or vanilla rice/coconut/almond/soy/hemp milk, 1 handful dried apricots chopped, 1 handful dried cranberries chopped, 1 teaspoon all-spice or cinnamon.

Preparation: Bring the water to a boil and pour in the rice, bring to a boil, reduce the heat to low, and cook according to package directions for time. After cooking the required time, keep the rice on low heat and add the 3 ounces of plain or milk, stirring in, and then letting it cook in until absorbed. When fully absorbed, pour in a bowl, add the dried apricots, and cranberries, and sprinkle with either all-spice or cinnamon. Enjoy! This is yummy!

It is a great experience to be able to consciously make decisions about what you want for yourself in your life!

1 cup tea optional

Lunch: Romaine Wraps

Ingredients: 2 romaine lettuce leaves, 4-6 stalks grilled asparagus (or whatever you have left from yesterday), 6 ounces broccoli or cauliflower steamed or raw, 1 bell pepper any color cut into slices, 2 ounces peanut or sesame dressing (recipes listed at the end)

Preparation: You can leave the broccoli or cauliflower raw if you prefer. If not, then steam it. In a medium-size pot, bring 2 cups of water to a boil. Put the cut-up stalk of either broccoli or cauliflower in the boiling water, and steam covered for 2 minutes. Stir another 2 minutes. This should leave the veggies crunchy. You can check the texture with a fork.

Wash 2 romaine lettuce leaves and pat dry. Using half of the ingredients on each piece of romaine, layer on the asparagus, broccoli or cauliflower, and bell pepper. Drizzle the peanut or sesame dressing over the veggies and roll it up, and eat.

Dinner: 17-Bean Soup

Stores carry a package called "17 Bean Soup," which is a blend of beans. If your local store does not carry this then make a blend of beans yourself, using cannellini beans, kidney beans, black beans, split peas, orange lentils, yellow lentils, pinto beans, adzuki beans, and garbanzo beans. Some stores even carry this bean mix in their bin section.

Ingredients: one 16-ounce package of 17-Bean Soup, 2-3 liters of water, 2 tablespoons extra-virgin olive oil, ½ -1 cup diced carrots, ½ -1 cup diced celery, ½ -1 cup red onions diced, 2 tablespoons minced garlic, 2 teaspoons cumin, 2 teaspoons cardamom, 2 teaspoons ground fennel, salt and pepper to taste

Preparation: If you did soak the beans, drain and rinse them, then set aside.

If you did not soak the beans overnight, there is only a little difference in the cooking. Put 3 cup of water in a pot with the beans, cover, and bring to a boil. Keep at a hard boil for 10 minutes covered. Then, reduce the heat so the beans are simmering. Simmer covered for about 30 minutes or until the beans are tender. Drain the beans after this quick soak, discarding the water.

Crock pot preparation: In a crock pot drizzle in the olive oil, add the carrots, celery, red onions, and garlic, and mix together to coat all with the olive oil. Let this cook for 1 hour on high. After 1 hour, pour in the beans, sprinkle on the cumin, cardamom, ground fennel, salt, and pepper, cover with water, and stir all the ingredients. Reduce to low heat if it will be cooking for 6 hours, keep at high heat if cooking for 4 hours.

Crock pot variation If you need to, put all the ingredients in the crock pot at the same time and head out the door. It will still be wonderful!

Stovetop preparation: In a large pot on high heat, drizzle in the olive oil, add the carrots, celery, red onions, and garlic in and mix together so the veggies are coated with the olive oil. Sauté on medium heat for about 10 minutes, stirring every 2-3 minutes to keep the vegetables from burning. Pour in the beans, sprinkle on the cumin, cardamom, ground fennel, salt, and pepper, cover with water, cover with a lid, and increase the heat to high to bring to a boil. Once boiling, reduce heat so that the beans just simmer, and cook covered for about 3 hours, or until all the beans are tender.

"I feel good!"

_____

_____

_____

_____

_____

_____

_____

_____

_____

Day 28

Breakfast: 12 ounces water

Power Toast

Ingredients: 2 piece of wheat-free bread (kamut, spelt, rye, or multigrain), 2 teaspoons peanut butter, 1 banana sliced, and protein smoothie of your choice (all the smoothie recipes are listed at the end)
Toast the 2 pieces of bread, spread with peanut butter, and layer banana slices on each piece. Make the protein smoothie of your choice.

This is the best way to make your life the story you WANT to tell!

1 cup tea optional

Lunch: Avocado, Fennel, and Tomato Salad With Balsamic Vinaigrette

Ingredients: 1 avocado diced, 1 fennel bulb diced, ½ cup tomatoes chopped, 2 ounces balsamic vinaigrette dressing (recipe listed at the end).

Preparation: Place all ingredients in a bowl, drizzle in the balsamic dressing, and toss together.

Dinner: Barley and Grilled Vegetables

Ingredients: ½ cup pearl barley, 1 cup water, 3 tablespoons extra-virgin olive oil, 7 pieces of asparagus, 1 bell pepper any color, 2 ounces pine nuts or almonds, 1 lemon juiced, ¼-½ teaspoon salt, 2 tablespoons flax or chia seeds ground

Personal favorite: I like to dry-roast grains before putting them in the boiling liquid. This cooks off some of the sugars. In a large skillet on high heat, pour the grains in, stir occasionally being careful not to burn them. Once all the grains are a light brown color, remove from the heat. They are ready to be poured into the boiling liquid for the next cooking step.

Preparation, barley: Pour the water into a pot, turn to high heat, drizzle in ½ teaspoon olive oil, and bring the water to a boil. Pour in the barley and stir, reduce the heat and cover, keeping at a simmer for 20-23 minutes or until the water is absorbed.

Preparation, grilled vegetables: Place the asparagus and bell pepper on a cookie sheet, drizzle with 2 teaspoons of olive oil, place under the broiler with the heat on high. Check every 5 minutes, and broil until slightly charred and rotate. Continue so that all sides of the asparagus and bell pepper are slightly charred.

Once they are cooked, put the grilled bell pepper in a brown paper bag. Let all of the vegetables cool. Once the bell pepper has cooled, remove it from the bag, and peel off the skin. (You can leave the skin on it is full of nutrients, but some people find at adds a slightly bitter taste.) Slit the bell pepper in half and remove the seeds and stem. Then cut the bell pepper and asparagus into bite-size pieces. **Option** to grill the whole bundle of asparagus. If you do, you can use the remainder in the next few days, even to enjoy on its own.

Preparation, nuts: Coarsely chop the almonds, if using. Set aside the almonds or the pine nuts.

Preparation, lemon juice mixture: Whisk together 2 tablespoons of the olive oil, the juice of 1 lemon, and ¼ teaspoon of salt, set aside.

Putting it all together: In a mixing bowl, place 1 cup of cooked barley, the asparagus and ½ bell pepper cut into bite-size pieces, the pine nuts or almonds. Pour on the olive oil lemon mixture, sprinkle with flax or chia seeds, toss together, then enjoy!

Night-Before Prep: Tomorrow's breakfast is muesli. Make it tonight, if this is easier, unless you have some left from Day 13

"I feel good!"

_____
_____
_____
_____
_____
_____
_____
_____
_____

Day 29

Breakfast: 12 ounces water

Muesli

Ingredients: 2 cups rolled oats, ½ cup barley flakes, 1 teaspoon canola oil margarine, ½ cup sunflower seeds, ¼ cup pumpkin seeds, ¼ cup pecans finely chopped, ¼ cup almonds finely chopped, ½ cup wheat germ, 2 tablespoons chia seeds, ½ cup shredded coconut, and ½ cup each of any 2 dried fruits diced, such as raisins, cranberries, apricots, blueberries, apples, pineapple, or mango

Preparation: Preheat the oven to 325 degrees. In a large mixing bowl combine the rolled oats and the barley flakes, mixing evenly. On a baking sheet, very lightly covered with canola oil margarine, spread the oat and barley mixture. Bake for 5 minutes, mixing it halfway through. Mix in the sunflower seeds, pumpkin seeds, pecans, and almonds, blending evenly. Return this to the oven for 5 more minutes, mixing halfway through. Remove from the oven and let cool. Mix in the wheat germ, chia seeds, coconut, and 2 dried fruits. Store this in an air-tight container.

This might become one of your favorite cereals to have around. It's a favorite in our house and we always have some stored. It is a great alternative to store-bought cereals with sweeteners that you really don't need.

You can enjoy this muesli as a hot cereal or cold cereal.

Preparation, hot cereal: Bring 1 cup of water to a boil, stir in 6 ounces of muesli and reduce heat to medium. Continue stirring, this will cook fast. Once the water is absorbed, it is done. You can sprinkle cinnamon or all-spice on top if you would like. This is really yummy!

Preparation, cold cereal: Place 6 ounces of muesli in a bowl and cover with a soy/rice/coconut/almond/hemp milk.

Granola as an option: If you are having a store-bought granola instead, keep in mind that most granolas do have a high amount of sugar, even though it is natural. Pour in your milk of choice. If the milk you are using is not an unsweetened, its addition to the granola will add to the sugar content of this breakfast.

Take a moment this morning to acknowledge the investment you are making in yourself!

1 cup tea optional

Lunch: Almond Butter Sandwich
This lunch was meant as a fun and easy alternative to some of the other lunches that take more time to prepare. This lunch is very easy to prepare and even to pack up to go. It is also great to try something this delicious and healthy as a way to see that you can incorporate this into your life even when you are done with this Full-Body Cleanse.

Ingredients: 2 piece of wheat-free bread (kamut, spelt, rye, or multigrain), 1-2 ounces almond butter. **Options:** pick 1: ½ apple sliced any color, or 2 ounces raisins, or 2 ounces dried cranberries, or 2 ounces dried pomegranate, or 2 ounces dried cranberries and dried pomegranate together

Preparation: Toast the bread slightly. Spread the almond butter on 1 piece and then top off with 1 of the fruit choices.

Dinner: Grilled Eggplant

Ingredients: 1 medium-large eggplant cut in slices (if you use Japanese eggplants, use 4-6), 1 tablespoon salt, 3-4 tablespoons sesame oil, sesame dressing (recipe from Day 2, also listed at the end).
Option to add tofu and/or red chili pepper flakes

Preparation: You can slice the eggplant into round slices, or longitudinally into lengthwise pieces. The pieces should be approximately ½-inch thick for easy grilling. After slicing the eggplant, place them on a cookie sheet, and sprinkle with salt. This pulls the water out of the eggplant, allowing for a shorter broiling time. The eggplant is ready to broil once it has begun to "sweat" (water drops will appear). Drizzle 1 ½ tablespoons of the sesame oil on one side of the eggplant, flip and drizzle the other 1 ½ tablespoons of the sesame oil on the other side. With the broiler on high, place the eggplant under the broiler for about 7 minutes, checking to make sure it doesn't burn. Once it is slightly charred, flip the pieces over and broil the other side until slightly charred. Let cool and then cut into bite-size pieces. Set aside.

Option to add sautéed tofu, which you may have left from Day 26 dinner. If not, cut a 14-ounce container of firm tofu into cubes. In a skillet on high drizzle in 1 tablespoons sesame oil, heat for about 1 minute, then add the cubed tofu, and reduce heat to medium-high and sauté for about 5 minutes, stirring at 1 minute intervals.

Putting it all together: In a mixing bowl place the bite-size pieces of eggplant, add the tofu if you opted for it, and chili flakes if you want. Drizzle on the sesame dressing, toss together, and enjoy.

Night-Before Prep: Tomorrow's dinner includes pasta sauce. If you want to make your own, it would be helpful to make it tonight, storing it in the refrigerator overnight. Tomorrow's dinner will be cooked in the crock pot for 3-5 hours, or on the stove top for 2 hours, which is why it would be helpful to have your pasta sauce ready in advance.

"I feel good!"

_____
_____
_____
_____
_____
_____
_____
_____

Day 30

Breakfast: 12 ounces water

Toast and Avocado

Ingredients: 2 pieces of wheat free bread (kamut, spelt, rye, or multigrain), 1 avocado, and 1 protein smoothie (choose from the smoothie list toward the end)

Preparation: Toast 2 pieces of the bread you are using. Slice the avocado lengthwise and place the slices on the toast. Make your smoothie. Enjoy a great breakfast that will supply you with solid nutrients and help you feel ready to get things done.

"Will you look back on life and say, 'I wish I had,' or 'I'm glad I did'?"- Zig Ziglar

1 cup tea optional

Lunch: Barley and Nuts
This is a nice hearty lunch that will give you a good pick-me-up to carry you through your day!

Ingredients: 1 tablespoon walnut or almond oil (if you don't have either, use extra-virgin olive oil), 5 mushrooms diced, 2 celery stalks diced, 1/8 teaspoon nutmeg (just a little pinch), 1 ¼ cups organic vegetable stock, ½ cup uncooked pearl barley, 1 ounce pecans chopped, 1 ounce sunflower seeds

Personal favorite: I like to dry-roast grains before putting them in the boiling liquid. This cooks off some of the sugars. In a large skillet on high heat, pour the grains in, stir occasionally being careful not to burn them. Once all the grains are a light brown color, remove from the heat. They are ready to be poured into the boiling liquid for the next cooking step.

Preparation: In a skillet on high heat pour the walnut, almond, or olive oil in and heat for 1-2 minutes. Add the mushrooms, celery, and nutmeg and sauté on medium for about 5 minutes, stirring occasionally. Pour the organic vegetable stock in and cover, increase heat to high, and bring to a boil. Add in the barley, pecans, and sunflower seeds. Bring to a boil, reduce heat so that the barley is only at a simmer, cover, and cook for about 20-23 minutes, or until all the vegetable stock is absorbed.

Dinner: Red Sauce and Veggies

Ingredients, pasta sauce: 2 tablespoons extra-virgin olive oil, 1 cup onions chopped, 4 cloves garlic diced, 25 ounces chopped tomatoes, 1.6-ounce can tomato paste, 1 teaspoon salt, ¼ teaspoon black pepper, ¼ teaspoon dried oregano, 12 organic fresh basil leaves chopped
Options: ½ - ¾ pound mushrooms chopped, 1 ounce balsamic vinegar, 1-2 ounces baby carrots chopped, pinch of red chili pepper flakes.

Ingredients, veggies: 2 tablespoons extra-virgin olive oil, 4-5 zucchini chopped, 2 medium red onions chopped (can substitute yellow onions if you want, but red are sweeter). If you want this to be a little heartier, add 2 regular-size potatoes, cut into pieces.

Option: 2 hours before eating you can add 1-2 bulbs of chopped fennel. Fennel is delicious in this dish, but it may not work with your schedule. This dinner is great without the fennel anyway.

Time-Saving Tip: You can buy one 25-ounce jar of organic pasta sauce, such as basil garlic sauce, but do not choose one with milk or cream listed in the ingredients.

Preparation, pasta sauce: Pour the olive oil in a large pot and heat on high. Add the onions and garlic, stirring, and reduce heat to medium for 10 minutes, stirring about every 2 minutes. Add the chopped tomatoes, tomato paste, salt, pepper, dried oregano, and any of the options you want, and bring to a boil. Reduce the heat so the sauce is simmering, and let simmer for 1-2 hours.

Putting it all together:

Crock pot preparation: In a crock pot, pour in the olive oil, layer in the zucchini on the bottom, then the onions. If you are using potatoes, place them in with all the ingredients at this time. Cover with the pasta sauce and cook on low for 5 hours, or high for 3 hours. Right before you will be serving this dish, sprinkle on the fresh basil leaves.
Option: If using fennel in this dish, add it to the sauce 1-2 hours before its done cooking.

Stovetop preparation: This is the same as for the crock pot, but you would keep everything on low heat covered for 2 hours. If you are using fennel add it to the sauce for the last 30 minutes.

"Your motivation will get you started. Then keep your motivation AND the new habits and continue on with a healthy lifestyle."– Ahnjel Ali

"I feel good!"

_____

_____

_____

_____

_____

_____

_____

_____

Congratulations!!!!
I truly hope you are feeling better than when you started this
30-Day Full-Body Vegan Cleanse. This material represents
how my family has lived for a number of years. We didn't
wake up one morning and have all of this in our heads. This
came about first by our conscious decision to keep ourselves
healthy through our lifestyle. Over the years, we have
experimented, shaped, and molded a very healthy lifestyle
that we sincerely enjoy living every day, and are very proud
of. You should feel pride in yourself for your accomplishment.
It does take work and conscious thought to eat the way you
just ate for these past 30 days.
Over the years, we have prepared many different types of
foods. All the recipes in this Cleanse are just some of the foods
we have cooked. All the smoothies have come about also as an
evolutionary process for us out of need for calories for
ourselves and as a way to get extra calories in our boys before
some of their athletic activities. As a family, we have also
enjoyed playing with combining different vegetables for some
refreshing and very healthy juices.
If you found it difficult because it is new to you, please know
that the longer you eat this way, the easier it becomes. I
sincerely hope you have discovered how wonderful it is to eat
in the healthiest way. I hope you can feel a big difference
throughout your whole body!

Snack Options

It would be best to eat a snack between your meals if you are hungry. If you do snack there are plenty of options. Within these options, always choose one snack from either the "vegetable/fruit" category or the "juices" category. By doing so, you will get an extra serving of a fruit or vegetables for the day while supplying your body with the most nutrients you can get from foods. The one other snack could be from the "other choices" category.

Vegetable/Fruit
- 1 bell pepper – red, orange, yellow, or green
- 1 cup sugar plum tomatoes
- ½ cup sugar snap peas
- ½ cup baby carrots
- 1 cup steamed green beans
- 1 cup steamed broccoli
- 1 cup steamed zucchini
- 1 sliced cucumber
- 1 cup jicama. I like to squeeze a lemon over my jicama, especially if I prepare it the night before. The lemon juice will keep it fresher. Adding a sprinkle of paprika is a really yummy option too.
- 1 cup steamed cauliflower
- 1 sliced apple with 1-2 tablespoons peanut or almond butter
- ½ cup baby carrots or carrot sticks with 1-2 ounces hummus
- 2 celery stalks with 1-2 tablespoons peanut butter or almond
- 4 plums
- ¾ cup watermelon/cantaloupe/honeydew
- 1 banana
- 1 orange or 2 tangerines

Any fruit or vegetable would be a great snack!

Other Snack Choices

- 15 rice crackers with 2 tablespoons of hummus
- 15 rice crackers with 2 tablespoons of olive tapenade
- 1 ounce any nuts – walnuts, cashews, almonds, Brazil nuts, peanuts, pistachios. This is usually about 1 handful.
- 1 ounce any seeds – sunflower, pumpkin. This is usually about 1 handful.
- Unique and Yummy Trail Mix – Blend together roasted cashews, dried cranberries, and dried pomegranate seed. This is awesome and will pick you up quick in the middle of the day. If you want to make this extra special, you can add a few carob chips.
- Almond Trail Mix – Blend together almonds, roasted soy nuts, chopped up dried apricots, and shredded coconut.
- Dried apples –Have up to 2 servings; 1 serving size of dried fruit is ¼ cup.
- Soy or almond yogurt –If you are in need of more calories than a yogurt will provide, try mixing some of your muesli into the yogurt.

Dressings

Balsamic Vinaigrette
Ingredients: ¼ cup balsamic vinegar, ½ cup extra-virgin olive oil, ¼ teaspoon salt, ¼ teaspoon black pepper, 1 clove garlic minced.
Optional: 1 tablespoon Dijon mustard; 1 teaspoon honey.
Preparation: Whisk all ingredients together. Refrigerate any unused portion. This will hold for two weeks.

Sesame Dressing
Ingredients: 1 tablespoon minced garlic, 1 tablespoon minced ginger, 3- 6 tablespoons Bragg's Liquid Aminos or tamari sauce (Try it with 3 tablespoons first, then add more for your taste preference.), 1 tablespoon rice wine vinegar, 1 tablespoon sesame oil, ¼ cup vegetable oil.
Optional: 2 tablespoons vegan mayonnaise, which will make it creamy
Optional: ¾ teaspoon red chili pepper flakes
Optional: 1 tablespoon honey
Preparation: Whisk all ingredients together until they are well blended. Refrigerate after use. This will hold for two weeks.

Peanut Dressing
Ingredients: ½ cup non-crunchy peanut butter, 2 ½ teaspoons sesame oil, ½ cup vegetable oil, 2 tablespoons tamari sauce, 1 tablespoon rice wine vinegar, 1 lime, 2 cloves of garlic chopped, 3 tablespoons honey, 1 tablespoon ginger chopped, ½ cup cilantro chopped, ¼ teaspoon salt, 3 tablespoons water
Optional: add 2-3 teaspoons of crushed red pepper.
Preparation: Place all ingredients in a blender or the Vitamix® and puree until creamy. Refrigerate after use. This will hold for two weeks.

Cilantro Dressing

Ingredients: 3 cloves of garlic chopped, 1 cup cilantro packed and chopped, ¾ cup parsley packed and chopped, 1 tablespoon minced fresh ginger, ¾ cup fresh lime juice, 1 tablespoon wine vinegar or apple cider vinegar, ¾ cup extra-virgin olive oil, ¼ -½ teaspoon salt, ¼ teaspoon pepper.

Optional: ½ -1 tablespoon honey (I prefer no sweetener at all, but others like it); 1 pinch of red chili pepper flakes

Preparation: Turn on food processor or the Vitamix®, add in the garlic, cilantro, parsley, and ginger. Process until finely chopped. Keeping the food processor on, add the lime juice, vinegar, olive oil, salt, pepper, and any of the options you want. Process until all has become a smooth creamy dressing. Refrigerate any unused portion. This will hold for two weeks.

Garlic Dressing

Ingredients: 6 tablespoons extra-virgin olive oil, ½ lemon juiced, 3 tablespoons red or white wine vinegar, 3 cloves garlic minced, ½ -1 teaspoon salt, 1/8 -1/2 teaspoon pepper

Optional: 2 tablespoons tamari sauce or Bragg's Liquid Aminos, or ½ - 1 teaspoon oregano

Preparation: You can either whisk the ingredients together or blend them in the blender or the Vitamix®. First, whisk or blend the olive oil, lemon juice, and vinegar until smooth. Then add in the remanding ingredients and again whisk or blend until smooth. Refrigerate if there is time before using. Store in the refrigerator any that is left. This holds for up to 2 weeks.

Juices

A Vitamix® is your best kitchen appliance for making the healthiest and most complete vegetable juices you can get. The Vitamix® is a very powerful blender that allows you to juice the entire plant. You end up extracting not just the juice from the plants, but also ALL the fiber and nutrients the plants have. And because you use the entire plant, you will need less of the ingredients than if you were just juicing. Nothing gets thrown away, as it does when using a regular juicer.

To order a Vitamix®, visit www.vitamix .com or call +1 800-848-2649. You can get free ground shipping by using the code 06-00749. That will be a savings of $25.00.

Using a regular juicer is the next best thing if you will be adding juicing to your Full-Body Cleanse.
Vegetable juices are preferred over fruit juices.

Spinach, Celery, Parsley, (SCP)

This is one of the best juices you could drink every day of this Full-Body Cleanse. Deep green vegetables are the best foods you can eat for your liver. Our liver is a very hard-working organ from even before your birth. The SCP recipe is listed below, followed by variations.
If SCP does not appeal to you, try instead the Kale juices. Kale is another deep green that provides great phytochemicals and antioxidants.

If using the Vitamix ® for all juice recipes, this is standard: Add 5 ice cubes into the Vitamix ®, then some of the chosen veggies and some water. Start the Vitamix ® on the low setting and then increase to setting 10. Keeping the setting on 10, remove the plastic portion of the lid, and through the hole begin adding in the rest of the vegetables. Once all the ingredients are in the Vitamix ®, flip the switch to high and blend for about 1-1 ½ minutes. While on high, you can add 4-5 more ice cubes and more water to end up with the Vitamix ® full to the top. This does yield a lot of juice; you can reduce the amount of the veggies and make less.

It's very important to add a "warm" ingredient to these juices. In all of these vegetable juices add two ingredients that are "warm" in nature. As an Acupuncturist and Chinese Herbalist, I am always striving for balance, which definitely applies to the foods I eat. In the Chinese Medical system, raw vegetables are "cold" in nature, and are very harsh to the digestive. Adding in a food that is "warm" dramatically helps your digestive tract to metabolize the food. Warm foods warm the stomach and intestines, eliminating the gas and bloating usually experienced from consuming raw vegetables. Garlic and radishes are warm in nature. One or both of these should always be used in these vegetable juices.

SCP: For Vitamix ®, ¼- ½ bunch spinach, 4-6 stalks celery, ¼- ½ bunch parsley, 1-2 cloves garlic, 4 radishes; double the spinach, celery, and parsley for regular juicer.

SCP and Carrot Tops: For Vitamix ®, ¼- ½ bunch spinach, 4-6 stalks celery, ¼- ½ bunch parsley, ½ bundle of carrot tops, 1-2 cloves garlic, 4 radishes; double the spinach, celery, and parsley for regular juicer.

SCP and Beet Tops: For Vitamix ®, ¼- ½ bunch spinach, 4-6 stalks celery, ¼- ½ bunch parsley, ¼- ½ bundle of beet tops, 1 - 2 cloves garlic, 4 radishes; double the spinach, celery, and parsley for regular juicer.

SCP and Beets: For Vitamix ®, ¼- ½ bunch spinach, 4-6 stalks celery, ¼- ½ bunch parsley, 1 beet, 1-2 cloves garlic, 4 radishes); double the spinach, celery, and parsley for regular juicer.

SCP and Carrots: For Vitamix ®, ¼- ½ bunch Spinach, 4-6 stalks celery, ¼- ½ bunch parsley, ½ cup baby carrots, 1-2 cloves garlic, 4 radishes; double the spinach, celery, and parsley and carrots for regular juicer.

SCP and Apple: For Vitamix ®, ¼- ½ bunch Spinach, 4-6 stalks celery, ¼- ½ bunch parsley, 1 apple, 1 -2 cloves garlic, 4 radishes; double the spinach, celery, and parsley for regular juicer.

Kale, Parsley, Cucumber and Watercress: For Vitamix ®, 2-3 kale leaves, ¼- ½ bundle parsley, 1 cucumber, 2-4 radishes, 1-2 cloves garlic; double all ingredients for regular juicer.

Kale, Parsley, Celery, Apple, and Watercress: For Vitamix ®, 2-3 kale leaves, ¼- ½ bundle parsley, 4-6 stalks celery, ½ apple, 2-4 radishes, 1-2 cloves garlic; double all ingredients for regular juicer.

Kale, Parsley, Apple, and Watercress: For Vitamix ®, 2-3 kale leaves, ¼- ½ bundle parsley, ½ apple, 2-4 radishes 1-2 cloves garlic; double all ingredients for regular juicer.

Kale, Parsley, Carrot, and Watercress: For Vitamix ®, 2-3 kale leaves, ¼- ½ bundle parsley, 1 carrot, 2-4 radishes, 1-2 cloves garlic; double all ingredients for regular juicer.

Cucumber, Apple, Carrot: For Vitamix ®, ½ cucumber, ½ apple, 1 carrot, 1-2 cloves garlic, 3 radishes; double all ingredients for a regular juicer. This is a very refreshing juice, and you can play with the proportions of each ingredient for your taste preference.

Beet, Celery, Arugula: For Vitamix ®, 1 red beet, 5 celery stalks, ½ bunch arugula, 1-2 cloves garlic, 4 radishes; double all ingredients for regular juicer.

This is not meant to be a complete list of the juices you can make, however it does list some of the best vegetable juices you can drink. The deep green vegetables are highly nutritious and beets are great blood cleansers. If you want more choices, there are numerous books available with lots of different juice recipes.

Protein Smoothies

You can bring protein smoothies into your diet in a number of ways. First, you can make them a part of a meal, having one with other food items for breakfast or lunch.

Secondly, you can drink one as a snack, for example, between breakfast and lunch.

I see protein smoothies as a way to consume healthy calories yet not as filling as a meal.

These are called "protein smoothies" because there's usually a protein source in them, but gauge this for yourself as to whether you need the extra calories from a protein powder or not. This will depend on your activity level. If you are working out, burning a lot of calories, and have a high output of calories throughout the day, then use 1 or 2 scoops of one of the protein powders listed below. If your energy output is not as high and you do not burn through as many calories, then make these without the protein powder.

Protein powders: Choose 1 or 2. In each smoothie, you can use 2 scoops of protein powder, either 1 scoop of 2 different protein powders or 2 scoops of the same one.

The best is **Juvo**, a vegan product made from 55 organic ingredients, therefore providing a vast array of phytonutrients.

Plant Basics by Lifetime: A very good product, clean, without added unhealthy ingredients.

Soy Essence, by Jarrow: Another very good product, clean and without added unhealthy ingredients.

NOTE: Adding a soy or almond yogurt is an option if you feel you will need some more calories in the smoothie. Depending on the smoothie you are making, you can either choose vanilla flavored yogurt, or one of the fruit flavors.

You can also add 1 teaspoon of flax seeds or chia seeds to your smoothies. It is a very easy way to get them in your diet.

Protein Smoothie Recipes

Note that you can play with the amounts of water and soy milk; you may prefer more soy milk and less water, or vice versa.

You can also replace the soy milk for unsweetened vanilla almond milk. Replacing with vanilla coconut milk, vanilla rice milk, vanilla almond milk, or vanilla hemp milk is also an option. Note, each of these has sugar and the unsweetened soy and the unsweetened almond milks do not, so any of these other replacements will make this smoothie sweeter. There is already a little sweetener in the protein powders and the banana makes it sweet too.

This is not meant to be a complete list of the smoothies you can make. There are books available on different smoothies; these are some of the ones I make for my family.

Chocolate Banana Smoothie: In a blender or Vitamix® place 1-2 scoops of a protein powder, 2 cups water, 1 cup unsweetened chocolate soy milk, ¾ frozen banana, 2 ice cubes. Blend until smooth and enjoy!

Vanilla Banana Smoothie: In a blender or Vitamix® place 1-2 scoops of a protein powder, 2 cups water, 1 cup unsweetened vanilla soy milk, ¾ frozen banana, 2 ice cubes. Blend until smooth and enjoy!

Chocolate Peanut Butter Banana Smoothie: In a blender or Vitamix® place 1-2 scoops of a protein powder, 2 cups water, 1 cup unsweetened chocolate soy milk, ¾ frozen banana, 1-2 tablespoons peanut butter (add up to 2 tablespoons if you really like peanut butter), 2 ice cubes. Blend until smooth and enjoy!

And just for fun you can replace the peanut butter with almond butter or cashew butter.

Vanilla Banana Peanut Butter Smoothie: In a blender or Vitamix® place 1-2 scoops of a protein powder, 2 cups water, 1 cup unsweetened vanilla soy milk, ¾ frozen banana, 1-2 tablespoons peanut butter (add up to 2 tablespoons if you really like peanut butter), 2 ice cubes. Blend until smooth and enjoy!

And just for fun you can replace the peanut butter with almond butter or cashew butter.

Berry Blast Smoothie: In a blender place or Vitamix® 1-2 scoops of a protein powder, 2 cups water, 1 cup unsweetened vanilla soy milk, 2 ounces frozen mixed berries (strawberries, blueberries, raspberries), ¾ frozen banana, 2 ice cubes. Blend until smooth and enjoy! A fruit-flavored soy or almond yogurt makes this even better!

Tropical Chill Smoothie: In a blender or Vitamix® place 1-2 scoops protein powder, 2 cups water, 1 cup unsweetened vanilla soy milk, 2 ounces frozen mango, 2 ounces pineapple, 2 ice cubes. Blend until smooth and enjoy! A fruit-flavored soy yogurt works great here.

Orange Plus Smoothie: In a blender or Vitamix® place 1-2 scoops protein powder, 2 cups orange juice, ¾ frozen banana, 2 ounces pineapple, 2 ounces frozen mixed berries. Blend until smooth and enjoy! A fruit-flavored soy or almond yogurt makes this even better!

Strawberry Pineapple Delight Smoothie: In a blender or Vitamix® place 1-2 scoops protein powder, 2 cups water, 1 cup unsweetened vanilla soy milk, 4 ounces frozen strawberries, 4 ounces pineapple. Blend until smooth and enjoy!

Amped Strawberry Pineapple Delight Smoothie: In a blender or Vitamix® place 1-2 scoops protein powder, 2 cups orange juice, 4 ounces frozen strawberries, 4 ounces pineapple. Blend until smooth and enjoy! A fruit-flavored soy or almond yogurt makes this even better!

Peachy Good Smoothie: In a blender or Vitamix® place 1 large peach and 1 large banana (if 1 of these can be frozen ahead of time it will make for a thick frosty shake), 2 cup water, 1 cup unsweetened vanilla soy milk. Blend until smooth.
Option to add peach soy yogurt, or almond yogurt, for more calories and a richer texture.

Shopping List

Alternatives for milk: unsweetened rice milk, unsweetened soy milk, unsweetened almond milk, unsweetened coconut milk.
If you absolutely cannot tolerate the unsweetened milks try the sweetened versions of rice milk, soy milk, almond milk, hemp, or coconut milk.

Butter substitutes: Earth's Balance Organic Buttery Spread is very good. Earth's Balance also now has a Coconut Organic Spread that is awesome!

Extra-virgin olive oil can replace butter on many things too.

Replace white sugar with stevia, agave, or sucanat. These are all natural sweeteners and are much better options if you need to add a sweetener to something, though there is nothing that really needs to be sweetened throughout this Cleanse.

Protein Powders: The best is **Juvo**, a vegan product made from 55 organic ingredients – vegetables, fruits, whole grains, sea vegetables, and mushrooms – therefore providing a vast array of phytonutrients.
Plant Basics, by Lifetime: A very good product, clean, without added unhealthy ingredients.
Soy Essence, by Jarrow: Another very good product, clean and without added unhealthy ingredients.

Peanut Butter: Organic is best, as these do not have any added sugar or oils. Trader Joes has a healthy peanut butter, and even a peanut butter with flax seeds.
Optional: Almond butter, cashew butter, or sunflower seed butter.

Bread alternatives: For this Cleanse, it would be best to eat breads that are wheat-free. The options are kamut, spelt, amaranth, quinoa, rice, and multigrain. NOTE: Most of these alternatives are pretty dense, so they are good and easier to eat of they are toasted!

Bob's Red Mills grain cereals. This company produces several different grain cereals for breakfast. These are excellent products and will all provide you with a variety of phytonutrients that your body needs. Take a look at all that this company makes and decide which ones you want to try.

Pasta, wheat-free pastas: spinach, rice, amaranth, corn pastas, spelt, potato blend. It truly is great that there are pastas available that are gluten-free. Most of these cook faster than the traditional wheat pasta, so read the label for cooking instructions and do not over-cook.

Yogurt: soy yogurts are good, just a little tangy, but easy to get used to. Almond yogurts are good too.

16313045R00085

Made in the USA
Charleston, SC
14 December 2012